"Thanks to Dr. Swenson for continuing to raise his voice in support of a more sane, more satisfying, more sustainable world. Overload and imbalance are neither desirable nor inevitable. Pushing back will move us forward. *In Search of Balance* offers both insights and strategies to take us to a better place."

—PATRICIA KATZ, productivity and balance strategist;
author of *Press Pause . . . Press On*

"I have benefited from the previous books by Richard Swenson on margin and overload, so I was excited to hear about *In Search of Balance*. In the midst of the aggressive progress of our age, we are no longer in tune with the rhythm of God's creation. Richard Swenson warns us about profusion and provides practical help in connecting balance (equilibrium) with margin (capacity)."

—KERBY ANDERSON, national director, Probe Ministries;
host, *Point of View* radio talk show

IN SEARCH OF
BALANCE

Keys to a Stable Life

RICHARD A. SWENSON, MD

NAVPRESS

DOWNLOAD
the free companion study guide at:

NavPress.com/insearchofbalance

NAVPRESS⬤

NavPress is the publishing ministry of The Navigators, an international Christian organization and leader in personal spiritual development. NavPress is committed to helping people grow spiritually and enjoy lives of meaning and hope through personal and group resources that are biblically rooted, culturally relevant, and highly practical.

For a free catalog go to www.NavPress.com
or call 1.800.366.7788 in the United States or 1.800.839.4769 in Canada.

© 2010 by Richard A. Swenson

All rights reserved. No part of this publication may be reproduced in any form without written permission from NavPress, P.O. Box 35001, Colorado Springs, CO 80935. www.navpress.com

NAVPRESS and the NAVPRESS logo are registered trademarks of NavPress. Absence of ® in connection with marks of NavPress or other parties does not indicate an absence of registration of those marks.

ISBN-13: 978-1-60006-698-6

Cover design by Arvid Wallen
Cover imagery by Shutterstock

Some of the anecdotal illustrations in this book are true to life and are included with the permission of the persons involved. All other illustrations are composites of real situations, and any resemblance to people living or dead is coincidental.

Unless otherwise identified, all Scripture quotations in this publication are taken from the *Holy Bible, New International Version*® (NIV®). Copyright © 1973, 1978, 1984 by International Bible Society. Used by permission of Zondervan. All rights reserved. Another version used is the King James Version (KJV).

Library of Congress Cataloging-in-Publication Data

Swenson, Richard A.
  In search of balance : keys to a stable life / Richard A. Swenson.
    p. cm.
  Includes bibliographical references.
  ISBN 978-1-60006-698-6
  1. Christian life. 2. Stress (Psychology)--Religious
aspects--Christianity. 3. Simplicity--Religious aspects--Christianity.
4. Time management--Religious aspects--Christianity. I. Title.
  BV4509.5.S945 2010
  248.8'619689--dc22
                                        2009045527

Printed in the United States of America

1 2 3 4 5 6 7 8 / 14 13 12 11 10

Dedicated To

Nico Everett Swenson

7-7-07 to 6-3-08

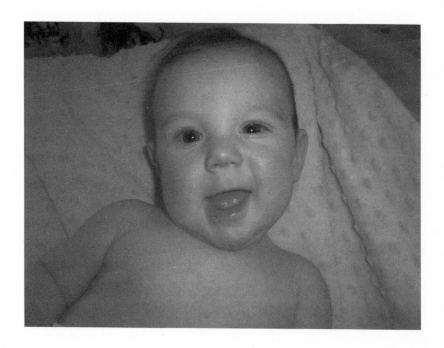

CONTENTS

ACKNOWLEDGMENTS

BOOKS ARE OFTEN written in a state of social isolation. Mine certainly are. Paradoxically, the process of researching and writing a book is also a profoundly social activity. It takes a legion to do the excruciating work of birthing a worthy volume. Laboring in obscurity, this noble crowd rarely receives recognition. Neither do they seek it. Yet it's always appropriate to honor those who work quietly in the shadows to benefit both author and reader.

First in line, as always, is my wife, Linda. She researches, copyedits, guides, and cheerleads; she smiles and grimaces at the correct times; and she somehow flexes with the bizarre biorhythm changes induced by a writing schedule. Her grace and patience keep an even keel in the midst of high seas, and it's hard to imagine any writing project, or life, without her at my side. Our two sons and their wives, Adam and Maureen and newly married Matt and Suzie, have again strengthened us with their steady support and encouragement. Katja Elizabeth Swenson, our granddaughter, deserves special thanks for her tender care of little brother Nico and for serving as a joy beacon when our spirits lagged. Thanks too for the prayers of family members Caroline, Mom, John, Don, Dad and Karen, Marcia and Jerry, Craig and Linda, Hazel, Paul and Comfort, Ron and Heather, and Tom and Vicki. Bless you.

From there the group expands like the roots of a tree. Gratitude flows to Jack and Diana Stimmel, Donna Knipfer, Bill and Gail Thedinga, Becky

Folkestad, Debbie Cowles, Aggie and Larry Wagner, Kris Brekke, Walter and Mary Schultz, Bob and Audrey Gayhart, Dan Harstad, Opal Harstad, Roger and Joanne Natwick, Hector and Betty Cruz, Beth and Willis Rubusch, Dr. Gene Rudd and the staff at CMDA, the Menomonie Public Library, and Martha, Dave, and Bob Stratton who provided inspiration for one portion of the text.

Beyond these names are another hundred who receive my writing and travel schedule. You shelter me with your thoughts and prayers, and I'm in your debt. Dr. Edwin Montell comforted our grieving hearts with his kindness upon the death of our grandson, and in a book dedicated to little Nico, I wish to thank him for his generosity.

Finally, to the staff of NavPress. Dan Benson's initiative was invaluable in placing this project on the launching pad. My wise editor and kind friend, Don Simpson, is always an honor to work beside. Mike, Kris, Tia, and all the rest—my thanks.

INTRODUCTION

CHAPTER

1

DREAMING THE POSSIBLE IMPOSSIBLE DREAM

"BALANCE IS BUNK!" screamed a title in the magazine *Fast Company*. "Living in a postbalance world" requires that we should "embrace imbalance" and become "happy workaholics."

The global economy is antibalance . . . Someday, all of us will have to become workaholics, happy or not, just to get by . . . Great leaders, serial innovators, even top sales reps may be driven by a kind of inner demon—the need to prove themselves . . . anxiety is a central part of our existence . . . Can any couple facing two full-time jobs, kids, aging parents, groceries, the dog, the bills, and telemarketers at dinnertime expect anything but all stress, all the time? . . . successful professionals found ways to switch the focus of their full attention with lightning speed among activities and people in different realms . . . Consider it an exercise in continuous redesign, in adapting to ever-changing circumstances and priorities. For couples, this also requires constant rebalancing of roles and responsibilities . . . Those who succeed are the people who learn to dance with change . . . They don't make decisions once or twice, but all the time.[1]

This particular author is not alone. "I really dislike the phrase work-life balance," wrote a female scientist, who nevertheless traveled overseas for her prestigious degree and career precisely so she could experience a better balance between career and family. "Balance is impossible," began a state supreme court judge's presentation on the tension between personal and professional life. "Balance is an excuse for noninvolvement, for not doing your best," said a Christian leader.

"Accept the craziness of your life," writes a prominent leadership trainer in the *Harvard Management Update*. "Do what you can do now. Let go of everything else."[2]

So, balance is now an impossible, bunk of an excuse for being a bum. And craziness is the new normal.

I wonder if the scoffers carry their thesis into other areas of life. Do they vote for the party with the least fiscal restraint because balancing the budget has no standing as a concept? Do they use their checkbooks with a similar casualness? Do they say to their pistons and spark plugs, "Feel free to do your own thing, don't worry about the other guys in there, I'm OK and you're OK, timing will fend for itself, and the engine won't mind"? Do they tell their thyroid that it is acceptable to be hypo and their blood pressure that it is hip to be hyper?

I am amazed at how quickly some have given up the battle for balance. A few have even trivialized it as a convenient fiction for the weak who do not wish to do the difficult work of life. Others have dumbed it down or redefined it into a shadowy principle that is as unrecognizable as it is ineffectual. Still others maintain that balance is, frankly, an impossible dream. It's both unrealistic and unattainable—and possibly even undesirable.

The trouble with simply giving up the struggle, throwing in the towel, and accepting an all-stress-all-the-time lifestyle is that it won't stop there. If we yield to the cultural treadmill, it will push us first into mild imbalance, then moderate imbalance, then severe imbalance, then beyond. Many are apparently unaware that we are waist deep in a dynamic situation where imbalance will continually escalate unless resisted. This is not a fight to be abrogated unless we don't care about the consequences of continuously worsening dysfunction.

Not to romanticize the past, but in 1960 most individuals, families, and workers were able to achieve some level of balance. Now, fifty years later, these same people find it difficult to achieve. What happened? Between 1960 and 2010, what pushed us—individuals, families, the workplace, and, indeed, the entire society—so forcefully in the direction of disequilibrium? The full explanation will be dealt with later in the book, but for now I wish to propose a more limited query. Regardless of what process caused this imbalancing momentum, do we have evidence that it has now finished its work and is prepared to leave us alone so we might reestablish a new equilibrium? On the contrary, the proliferation and profusion phenomenon that brought us to this place will only continue to accelerate. Any thought to the contrary reveals an underlying naïveté concerning the powerful forces that propel us forward.

Let me make the same point from a different direction. An eighteen-year medical study "Adherence to Healthy Lifestyle Habits" in *The American Journal of Medicine* examined five health habits and reported steadily worsening behaviors: the percentage of those with overweight body mass increased 8 percent, those with moderate alcohol use increased 11 percent, those achieving physical activity twelve times per month decreased 10 percent, and those eating five or more fruits and vegetables per day decreased 16 percent. Of the five monitored, the only lifestyle habit that did not worsen was cigarette smoking, holding steady at 26 percent (hardly qualifying as a victory).[3] Should we deduce from this study—and nearly every other study on this topic—that it is impossible for people to comply with healthy lifestyle habits and therefore we should all quit trying? Let's just cozy up on the sofa with our chips and dip and watch another movie marathon.

Trends in marriage are another illustration. Over the past several decades, many sociologists have asserted that the frequency of divorce and subsequent dissolution of families is now so commonplace that we should stop fighting it. Let's just accept this modern development and move to lessen the pain. Simply stated, this theory asserts that our age is inevitably driven by forces that uproot families and make people unable to remain together. The fast-paced requirements of our continuously changing culture have antiquated the "till death do us part" vow.

Consider, for example, the rather sensational divorce announcement of Sandra Tsing Loh in the *Atlantic* article "Let's Call the Whole Thing Off" (gruesomely subtitled "The author is ending her marriage. Isn't it time you did the same?").

> Given my staggering working mother's to-do list, I cannot take on yet another arduous home- and self-improvement project, that of rekindling our romance . . . And along the way, I've begun to wonder, what with all the abject and swallowed misery: Why do we still insist on marriage?[4]

In other words, the sooner we accept that marital harmony is mostly a mirage, the sooner we can decompress all the stress. "Family phase-two" means we will now have "serial marriages" and "temporary marriages" and our children will grow up with a big friendly group of semi-siblings.

But is the solution really to define away the pain rather than to counter the forces that cause the pain? The breaking up of families is *inherently* painful. This is not a wound because judgmental pulpit-pounders manipulate guilt. It is a wound because it is a wound. Ought we not work to strengthen the sustainability of love rather than justify the tenuousness of modern relationships?

Forgive me if either of these illustrations is uncomfortable—that is not my intention. I only wish to point out that many problems in life are best served by solving them rather than yielding to them. Balance is one such issue.

Thankfully those who have caved to the imbalance-is-inevitable view do not represent the majority opinion. The great preponderance of breathless moderns understand intuitively that balance is not only important but critical for healthy living. And they are willing to fight for it if given direction.

To be fair, the scoffers add some important correctives to this topic. Many of their concerns will be discussed at appropriate points later in the book, and at that time I'll gladly thank them for their contributions. As they point out, there is indeed much unrealistic thinking and simplistic analysis about the balance doctrine, and many of the resultant interventions seem inadequate. In addition, there are occasions when imbalance is expected and even helpful. At such times, appropriate imbalance can test us, discipline us, fortify us, and cause us to grow.

But to cut to the core, despite confusion and a few high-strung naysayers, balance is crucial. It always has been, and it always will be. Yes, balance has become *more* difficult to achieve—without a doubt. But if anything, balance is more important today than ever precisely because it's been wrenched away from so many of us with such dramatic force. When someone carjacks our vehicle, we tend to want it back rather than simply normalize our new walking blisters.

Balance Matters

In tracking this discussion and debate, it is interesting to note three recurring themes:

1. There is a *great deal of concern* about life balance today, much of it bordering on desperation. We witness this in magazines and books, in casual conversations and emails, in conference presentations, in family dynamics, and especially in the work environment.
2. There is a *great deal of confusion* about how to approach balance—even how to think about it, let alone achieve it.
3. There is a *great deal of evidence* that the requirement for balance exists far beyond the context of our busy lives, extending into every facet of existence.

To illustrate the imperative of balance, let's take a quick tour of the universe, from large to small, organic and inorganic, social sciences and physical sciences, and beyond. Pick up any rock in the universe and we will find the principle of balance inside, winking back at us. From the quantum structure of subatomic particles to the entire breadth of the cosmos itself, the balance of the universe is at a level that staggers comprehension. The human body has an inherent and inviolable demand for balance called homeostasis. Speaking as a physician, let me strongly suggest you not fall outside the parameters of homeostasis or you will quickly encounter both pain and expense.

We speak of balancing our budgets: corporate, personal, family, city, state, federal, and international. We are encouraged to eat a balanced diet. Knowing that falls are one of the biggest enemies of the elderly, we seek to find ways to maintain their balance and equilibrium. We laud an ecological balance and a balance of nature. Farmers are advised to practice a balanced crop rotation. Pilots and airlines are responsible for determining the appropriate weight balance in airplanes lest they fall suddenly from the sky. Our constitution guarantees a balance of power in the government, and we likewise desire an international balance of power to stabilize the prospects for global peace. Researchers and policy setters seek to balance risk versus benefit. We balance the tires on the outside of our automobiles and the stereos on the inside. Work-life balance in the marketplace has become such a widespread issue that it has spawned an entire industry to address it, with varying degrees of success.

We are surrounded, continuously, by the requirement for balance. Why, then, in our social infrastructure, is balance largely ignored? And as a spiritual principle, why is balance neglected and even scorned? In that regard, imbalance is like a flat tire, only showing up on our radar screen after we veer into a tree.

Blithely we heap more and more upon our already constrained twenty-four-hour days with a mysterious disregard for the consequences. And then we wonder when it was, exactly, that our lives spiraled out of control and our hope disappeared.

Sustainability in the Balance

A Phoenix builder told me of his prosperous commercial property development company that fell off a cliff in the 2008 global economic meltdown.

It took nine months before orders began to trickle in again. Then came the surprising part of his story. "You'd probably expect me to say how horrible this experience was," he said. "But when we hit the bottom, I can truthfully say that I didn't mind. Actually, I was glad. I was so burned out. Now after almost a year, I think I'm about ready to get back to work."

The man had a good job and a generous income. His company provided livelihoods for many workers. He had the privilege of driving around the city and pointing out all the tangible contributions he'd made to the growth of his community. But he could not sustain. The outflow exceeded the intake. The lack of balance caught up with him. I'm not referring here to the economic depression that brought him low—that crisis was international in scope and largely outside of his influence or culpability. Instead, I'm talking about his own internal emotional makeup. He'd simply run out of gas.

In a world where sustainability has become a rapidly moving target, balance provides a stabilizing influence. We might have the privilege of good work that we enjoy, yet, in today's whiplashing world, how many can sustain it over time without being stricken by that often-reported smoldering weariness? Those who are hyper-driven and rewarded by huge wealth seem best equipped to sustain the longest, perhaps simply because their internal intensity wiring and love of the bank ledger keep them energetic. Yet this same personality configuration is usually coupled with inadequate warning signals. They seldom realize when their limits have been exceeded. They also do not accurately understand that *all they are gaining* is being offset by *all they are giving up*. Balance keeps the needle set on the middle.

The focus of this book, of course, goes far beyond the elite of the corporate world. I'm equally concerned about the many well-intentioned working parents confronting screaming babies and smelly diapers in the middle of the night, knowing their alarms are set for 5:00 a.m. How are they going to sustain? What about the people-helping professions such as teachers, pastors, counselors, nurses, and doctors who have the double job of producing *and* relating? Or the farmers confronted with collapsing milk prices and no rain on the horizon?

Balance is not a panacea and it cannot work miracles. But balance can help people sustain in the midst of stress and overload by keeping the highs and lows from swinging wildly.

Balance can direct us toward simplified lifestyles, anchored contentment, nourished relationships, reasonable expectations, and manageable work. Balance can model for us the pace of faith with its gentleness and goodwill. Balance can equip us with a gyroscope that stabilizes our orbit securely around our timeless priorities. And, in the end, it's all about priorities.

Great Gifts or Grace?

"People with great gifts are easy to find," Emerson wrote, "but symmetrical and balanced ones, never." I wonder if we need more "great gifts" today, or if we need more grace? Where are the symmetrical, balanced people who are great because they have the time and energy to be kind?

The hunger of our day is not for inner-demon-driven, all-stress-all-the-time, switching-focus-at-lightning-speed, constant-rebalancing work-aholism—we already have literally millions of twitching rascals with prodigious productivity racing faster than photons. We have enough stuff, we have enough speed, we have plenty of progress, and we especially have a superabundance of *more*. But will you permit me to inquire about the status of our truth, love, faith, relationships, health, joy, depth, and peace? What corridor do we choose if we wish to rediscover the green pastures and still waters? What set of priorities will point us in that direction?

Balance is not the Kingdom, but if our priorities lie in that direction, balance can help us sustain our focus all the way Home.

PART ONE

HOW AGGRESSIVE PROGRESS SABOTAGES THE BALANCE WE NEED

WE LIVE IN a special moment in history and now sit upon a launch pad of unprecedented challenge and opportunity. It is a time of incredible transition. The global experience has grown massive in scope and nearly incomprehensible in complexity. Unrestrained profusion is exponential in the extreme and still accelerating. Mathematics has slipped its leash and was last seen going vertical. It is a day so unprecedented that even those who realize how unprecedented it is don't have a clue how truly unprecedented it is.

It is exciting. Historic. Destabilized. We have a destabilized economy and a destabilized healthcare system within a destabilized society within a destabilized world. Nothing can continue to change in this kind of trajectory. It's not possible.

This is not to say that we are in trouble, but it is to freely admit that we are troubled—and so we ought be watchful. Since the world system has never been here before, we do not know what is around the next bend. With a mixture of anticipation and anxiety, many of us swallow a tranquilizer and then, on tiptoes, slip an eyeball around the corner straining to get a peek. For me, peeking around the corner—or, more accurately, watching from the wall—has been my calling since 1982.

And balance? How has our good friend balance fared under the assault of such destabilizing change? It has been decimated.

Trading the White Coat for the Wall

I loved medicine and was a good physician, but medicine was not the reason I was put on the earth. Please do not misunderstand—I appreciated the privilege of being a doctor and the honor of serving wounded humanity in this special ministry. I did well within the profession, in both private practice and academics, and won some awards along the way. I loved my patients and was loved in return. The level of societal reimbursement was high, and I've never been sued.

Following years of dedicated training, I joined a multi-specialty clinic in an almost perfect Wisconsin setting, assuming this address would remain unchanged far into the sunset of my career. It didn't work out that way. In 1982, after only five years, the realization struck that private practice was not my precise calling. Significant changes ensued—I entered an academic teaching position, cut my work hours, and began an epic study project. The focus: everything. I am a natural integrationist by inclination, and so I undertook a study of the entire world system to trace how everything was connected to everything else. In the decade that followed, I gladly gave ten thousand hours to this endeavor, reading in the areas of education, economics, ethics, government, history, environment, health care, sociology, psychology, law, philosophy, the physical sciences, and future studies. In addition, my wife, Linda, contributed another five thousand hours of research. It was an intellectual feast. After a medical presentation in Seattle, one doctor asked, "Were those unreimbursed hours?" We could only laugh at such a totally foreign concept.

I worked as a clinical professor within the University of Wisconsin system for fifteen years while, off on a side track, I continued researching the times. Just as with private practice, my tenure of academic medicine went well. I enjoyed teaching, and the young physicians were a delight.

Nevertheless, it became increasingly apparent that my calling in life still had not been fully achieved. Twenty years into my medical career, I now knew that the reason I was born—my *raison d'être*—was to discern rather than to doctor. My calling was to be a discerner of the times, a futurist. The shingle on my door was supposed to read: *Watchman on the Wall*.

Many feel uncomfortable with the notion that somehow we are called or ordained with a certain gifting or predisposition. After presenting at a medical event, I was discussing the "calling" of medicine with a U.S. congressman (politicians sometimes value appearances at medical banquets because physicians are a good constituency, and the food's not bad either). "I don't believe in the idea of a calling," he said. "You find a job you're interested in and do it until it's over." Well, I'm not prepared to debate the point as it applies to others, but I can say with complete certitude that I was *born* to do this work. I was born trend-perceptive. My internal wiring, connected by God Himself, predisposed me in this direction.

I engaged in discerning the times with as much attention as my academic load would permit. But even though my work arrangement provided significant latitude—much more than most physicians—still it was insufficient. Consequently, in 1997, I resigned from the university system and left medical work entirely. Stepping away from the advantages of a physician's life is not easy, but there was never any question, really, of the course I would take. On the one hand, this shift deprived me of the many privileges medicine afforded. But, on the other hand, my decision allowed the freedom to stand on the wall twenty-four hours a day and analyze the torrent of incoming trends and signs. Even when asleep, I'm scanning the horizon. It is impossible for me to shut it down, and I don't even try.

I was now on the path laid out for me. Come what may, it was assuring to know my feet were on the right road traveling in the right direction for the right purposes. It would be correct to say *this is what I do*, but much more correct to say *this is who I am*.

Futurism is not mysticism, crystal-ball gazing, or New Age hocus pocus. It's integration. It's first collecting the trends and then connecting the dots. It's understanding the times as the Old Testament passage commends—the "men of Issachar, who understood the times and knew what

Israel should do."[1] But perhaps, most essentially, it's mathematics. In case you haven't noticed, the math is different today. This new math is both accelerated and stratospheric. One editorialist remarked, "I've lost track of the zeros." Exactly.

For three decades now, watching the unfolding story of history has been my privilege. It's always been a fascinating business. But what's coming at us now—what's just now rising above the horizon and headed our way—well, I've never seen anything like it.

A Brief Trip in a Time Machine

The world did not always behave this way—conditions were not always this destabilized, and the mathematics was not always escalating wildly. The drama I'm referring to here essentially unfolded in just the past three or four decades. When history decided to explode, it chose to do so on our generational shift.

What happened? Why are we visited with such unprecedented change? Is it a force for good, or is it an ill wind? To understand what happened, how it pertains to progress, and, importantly, why it sabotages balance, we must first take a brief stroll through the corridors of time.

The Past 5,000 Years

Recorded history began five millennia ago with the Sumerian cuneiform writing of the thirtieth century BC. If this sounds vaguely familiar, Sumeria is the area in modern-day Iraq where the patriarch Abraham, originator of the Hebrew race, first lived, the area of Ur of the Chaldees. The Sumerians were an advanced people in many ways, and, in addition to other accomplishments, they were the first to make a written record of their times.

Throughout the subsequent five millennia, bookkeepers, accountants, and various recorders scratched away on their stones, clay tablets, and parchments: triumphs—tragedies—invasions—conquests—consolidations—revolutions—explorations—discovery—growth—destitution—plagues—unspeakable horrors. If this seems to you an impressive list of exciting historical activity, you would be wrong. For most people living in this great span of time, life was slow, simple, and sad. Shakespeare's Macbeth characterized it well: "Tomorrow, and tomorrow, and tomorrow, Creeps in this petty pace from day to day, To the last syllable of recorded time."[2]

Balance issues existed to some extent perhaps, but they were not moving targets. No one would buy a book on the topic because there were more important issues to consider. Actually, no one would even think about balance because the word had no reference point.

If we took a "picture of balance"—a snapshot—5,000 years ago or 1,000 years ago, the image would be sharp and clear. There would be no movement whatsoever. Sneaking up through the woods and around buildings to get an unsuspecting shot, we would catch balance sitting on a stump, bored and unchanging. The masses passed by daily, never giving a thought to this unnamed visage sitting idly by himself.

To be sure, people in the distant past lived difficult lives, but every day was difficult in the same way as every other day. Difficult lives are not the same as unbalanced lives. Any imbalance was a static imbalance, and thus it would be accommodated. Each day would be difficult in the same way as the day before: the work would be long, the food short, health would be bad, teeth would fall out, animals would get sick, roofs would leak, locusts would eat the crops, and rats the bread.

Obviously, I do not wish to return to the era of rats and locusts. But I do wish to make the important point that life in antiquity—as miserable as it was—did not change much. Because the conditions of living changed so slowly, the issue of balance also changed slowly. People had time to accommodate to the conditions, therefore blunting much of the psychic trauma associated with tragedy and hardship. When we align expectations with reality, our internal mechanisms begin to accept hardship as the norm. And, believe it or not, people did find their own sources of friendship, laughter, beauty, and grace.

Yes, of course, family members died suddenly—but that was always the case. Just because they died suddenly did not mean that anything changed. People dying suddenly was an unchanging reality. Tragedy and destitution were everyday normal and so were factored in. You were hurt by it, but you were not surprised by it. Change happened slowly, if at all. The day people were born was largely identical to the day they died.

A slow pace of change always benefits balance by giving it a chance to adapt. But "slow pace of change" is a phrase that disappeared with the rats and the locusts.

The Past 250 Years

Let's get out the camera again and take another "picture of balance," this one 250 years ago. Here we begin to notice something different. There is a slight blurring of the image, and we realize that our subject is moving. It lurched. Life began to change, and with it, balance also was required to change. At first the movement was sluggish, and balance easily adapted. In addition, the change was largely for the better—this too benefited balance. People began to take notice of the improvement, and perhaps for the first time, in a longitudinally sustainable way, the change brought a glimmer of hope.

Progress had arrived and was about to take over.

Progress is the generalized notion that life improves. If people begin to lead healthier lives, this is called progress. If they make more money at their jobs, if they are able to afford better food, build bigger houses, and have more education, this too is called progress. As long as the arrows point up, as long as we get more and not less, we call it progress.

Of course, the onset of modern progress was not a flash of glorious light that swept away destitution overnight. Instead, the beginning was slow. But if it was slow, it was also deep, and once rooted nothing could stop it.

Perhaps we should begin with the Enlightenment, roughly dated 1650–1800. To be frank, as a Christian, I have significant disagreements with many Enlightenment thinkers, philosophies, and consequences—particularly its commonly expressed scorn of religion and transcendent truth. But on the positive side of the ledger, it should be acknowledged that the Enlightenment espoused ideas of universal education, liberty, democracy, self-governance, individual rights, tolerance, and the scientific method. For progress, it was a beginning.

Mostly, however, the cause of progress was advanced by the Industrial Revolution, roughly dated 1700–1900. This era was nothing less than an upheaval in all that came before, an explosion of possibility and productivity. It produced (in approximate chronological order) the first steam engine, power loom, cotton gin, electric motor, steamboat, locomotive, rail service, transatlantic steamship service, refrigeration, oil well, telegraph, transatlantic cable, telephone, incandescent lightbulb, diesel engine, wireless radio, dynamite, and manned flight. Even though Gutenberg's moveable-type printing press had been in use since 1440, the Industrial Revolution provided the means for the widespread dissemination of books and pamphlets. The quantum shift that flowed from such unprecedented technologies exceeded, by far, the accumulated advancement of the previous 5,000 years.

Changes in economics also folded into the mix. In 1776, Adam Smith became the father of modern economics with the publication of his *Wealth of Nations*. This was the first major work of systematic economics to be published, and it laid the foundation of modern economic science. In these five volumes, the Scottish moral philosopher expounded that the free market, open competition, and individual self-interest were guided by an invisible hand to produce the greatest benefit for the greatest number of people. Smith, in essence, provided the intellectual precursor for capitalism. The timing was perfect, for economic expansion was also aided by the Industrial Revolution's rising efficiency in production and the rapid increase in variety of goods available.

Developments in health care augmented the overall picture of improvement. In the 1840s, general anesthesia was used for the first time, initially with ether and then the less-dangerous chloroform. Overnight, surgery was revolutionized. Also in the mid-1800s, Hungarian obstetrician Ignaz Semmelweis, French microbiologist Louis Pasteur, and English surgeon Joseph Lister discovered—in a stunning development—the germ theory of disease. Concurrently, the related science of vaccination began eradicating dreaded infectious illnesses. Modern medicine was born.

As a direct result of these epic developments, change throughout the West was accelerating, making the era from 1750 to the present a time set apart. This modern 250-year segment of time has witnessed more change and progress than all previous millennia combined. Much more. More has happened to more people, more has been learned and earned, more has been discovered and taught, more has been piled up and piled on—more mobility, more media, more work, more technology, more education, more information, more travel, more communications, more weaponry, more possessions, more speed, more of everything.

To be sure, there were periods of accomplishment and even grandeur prior to 1750 but nothing even remotely approximating the explosion of progress over this past 250 years. Our recent past not only dwarfs our distant past, it annihilates it.

The above discussion, which we might label The Story of Progress, is obviously abbreviated, but it lays the necessary foundation for our next step. It is only by understanding how progress got its start and why it became so powerful that we are prepared to examine why progress has now become a problem—one that often complicates our lives, accelerates everything it touches, and sabotages the balance we need. Balance was first benefited by progress and then, more recently, devastated by the same force.

The story of *progress* now morphs to become the story of *more*.

More and More

Progress always leads to *more*. Always. Initially, it was the type of *more* that people wanted and needed. Eventually it evolved into a different kind of more, the kind that leads to overload and imbalance. But we are getting ahead of the story.

As progress took root in the 1700s and 1800s, it was natural for those living under its banner to develop an appreciation for its benefits. It's pleasing to have more bread and jam, plus a nickle to spare. It's encouraging to add a small room on the house for the children who didn't die from the epidemic that didn't happen. And, of course, it's particularly charming to have your abdominal abscesses lanced under general anesthesia.

and 'rithematic. Now, we can choose from over 500 college bacca-
laureate degrees available.

Proliferation—Once something is differentiated, progress will pro-
liferate it to whatever the market can bear. For example, once we differentiate
the dough into bagels, we can bake a million and sell them by noon.

Combination—The FDA approves only fifteen to thirty new molecu-
lar entities every year. Most other new pharmaceuticals on the market are
either combinations or differentiations of previous chemical structures.

Invention—Since 1790, the U.S. Patent Office has issued over seven
million patents for inventions. Much of our nation's corporate Research
and Development budget goes for invention, combination, or differentiation activities.

Discovery—Millions of new discoveries are logged every year—some
at great expense, others quite randomly—in areas such as chemistry,
physics, optics, astronomy, mathematics, biology, medicine, dentistry,
pharmacology, botany, zoology, metallurgy, electronics, economics, arche-
ology, history, sociology, anthropology, criminology, oceanography, mete-
orology, climatology, and space exploration.

It is easy now to see how progress generates *more*. Even a cursory
reading of this list explains the process. It's impossible to employ differentiation, proliferation, combination, invention, and discovery and end up
with *less* or the *same*. The process always leads to *more*. Even an economic
recession does not stop this process. Progress continues to give us more
but just at a slower rate.

The entire production of abundance has become almost routine,
effortless, and self-replicating. Once progress lines up the necessary conditions, it's a simple matter of pouring raw materials into the process and
then shipping the product to international markets. We begin with dough
or trees, and we end with riches.

We owe much to progress, and it knows it. Progress has spent hundreds of years perfecting its craft and is now in charge of not only the West
but increasingly portions of the entire globe. Sensing its preeminent position in today's order, progress wants increased recognition, responsibility,

and power. Since we, too, have larger appetites, we're only too pleased to feed progress the steroids it demands. Consequently, the ultramodern version of progress has advanced beyond just *more*. Now it gives us

more and more of everything faster and faster at exponential rates.

It's almost time to be worried.

The Past Thirty Years

Let's break out our camera for a final "picture of balance," this time in a contemporary setting. The result shows a complete blurring of the image, the kind that indicates rapid motion. We're not talking about a moving hand, or someone walking, or even a bounding gazelle being chased by a cheetah. This is more like a bullet in a wind tunnel.

As you might guess, balance today has a speed problem. The trouble is, balance and speed are about as harmonious as tofu and gasoline. The culprit is progress.

Progress has performed admirably for several hundred years, but the recent past has seen a spectacular run. Over the past thirty years there has been a crux point in the graphs when the direction swings straight up. Every corridor we explore reveals continuous acceleration, rapid change, wild gyrations, staggering complexity, huge numbers, and math that often does not work. Much of the responsibility for this can be laid at the feet of uncontrolled profusion.

As we shall see, the profusion curve for the past two thousand years is rather eye-catching. Let me introduce this phenomenon by comparing it with a mathematical illustration. If we double (fold) a piece of paper ten times, it will be two inches thick. If we double it forty times, it will go from here to the moon. If we double it one hundred times, it will extend to the far wall of the universe.

Welcome to the mathematical reality of modern profusion.

Profusion is defined as the generalized phenomenon of *more*. As we've already discussed, the world of the recent several hundred years is always, and unavoidably, experiencing an ever-increasing profusion. Mostly, profusion comes from progress. Where progress is most active, profusion is most active. We can even say that profusion is a function of progress.

Might it be possible to measure this profusion, perhaps even on a global scale? In order to do this, we would need to count all the people, all the products, all the technology, all the information and air miles traveled and toothpicks and everything else in the world. For the profusion measurement to be accurate, it must include millions of different categories:

> airbags, bowling balls, BlackBerrys, blackberries, turkeys, computers, nuclear weapons, credit cards, soybeans, lawsuits, lost luggage, ice cream cones, food additives, websites, kernels of corn, miles of highway, gallons of gas consumed, lightbulbs, movies, CDs, lawn mowers, clothes, taxes, books, golf balls, pagers, pieces of paper, cars, airplanes, money, debt, stores, hotels, ammunition, cigarettes, inventions, attorneys, magazines, pieces of mail, miles driven, miles flown, mortgages, houses, malls, energy used, missiles, catalogues, eggs, patents, laws, toys, telephones, televisions, overnight deliveries, offices, restaurants, guns, chemicals, cans of soda, copyrights

Finally, just when we are confident that nothing has been left out, we will remember a few last entries — key chains, coconuts, every grain of rice eaten by each person in Asia, every ounce of methane gas produced by cow flatus, every receipt from every department store. And, of course, every satellite orbiting, and every satellite dish, and every television program coming over each satellite dish, and every toggle switch in every spacecraft — John Glenn had 56 toggle switches in his first craft in 1962 and 856 in his second craft in 1998. We must not forget to include this increase.

Having accumulated every item in all of these millions of categories into one big pile, now let's attempt to measure it. Immediately, we see that measuring global profusion is literally impossible — it is too big, it is too inclusive, it changes too rapidly, there are no units to use, and there is no possible mechanism to collect all the data. But this in no way suggests that profusion is not a real objective quantity, only that it is too profound to measure in any practical sense. Yet, for the purposes of understanding how profusion changes over time, let's strain credibility and assume that we succeed in making our measurement.

Next, starting at the time of Christ, let's go back in history and measure the profusion for every year up to the present. Finally, let's construct a graph of the result.

The resultant graph would look like this:

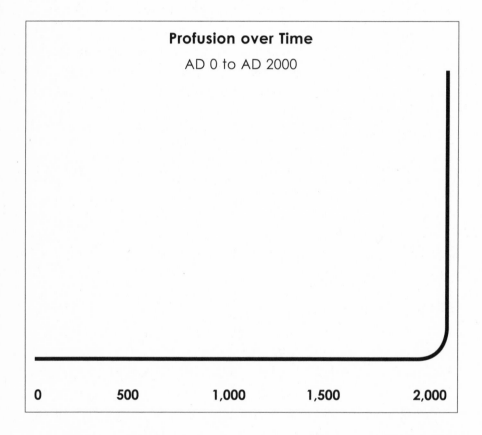

This graph is accurate.

I can hear you protesting. (And if you're not, you probably should be.) *Where is the profusion in AD 500, AD 1000, and AD 1500? Surely there was profusion all across the two-thousand-year time spectrum. Where is it? I don't see it indicated here.*

Yes, of course there was profusion in 500, 1000, and 1500, and, for that matter, in 1950. It is appropriately and accurately represented in the bottom of this curve as a straight horizontal line. The key to understanding this graph is in realizing just how mathematically massive profusion has been in the *most recent past*. The explosion of profusion during the last few decades forces all other numbers onto a flat line.

This graph IS correct.

Now, let's explore some implications and consequences.

1. Profusion climbs inexorably.

Profusion only goes in one direction: up. The rare exceptions to this rule are localized and temporary. Of course there will be decreases in the *rate of growth* of profusion, but it is important to notice that *this is not the same as profusion itself decreasing*. Even a prolonged recession does not destroy profusion but only slows its upward climb.

Perhaps we might best think of today's profusion as sitting atop a huge rocket blasting straight up, burning a billion tons of rocket fuel per second. If this illustration sounds like an exaggeration to you, then you still do not completely comprehend the mathematical physical reality of profusion.

2. Profusion is irreversible.

The phenomenon of profusion is irreversible because progress is a one-way street. The original engineers, it seems, forgot to install a reverse gear. As a result—for all practical purposes and for a multitude of reasons mostly involving the economy—the process of modernization is unidirectional. There is no turning back.

Regarding this irreversibility, progress can't help itself. It has only been taught to go in one direction—the direction of more and more of everything faster and faster. This is precisely what we have asked and expected of progress. Who in their right mind would expect progress to give us *less and less, slower and slower*?

3. Profusion is seen as a positive.

That the entire world system will experience an ever-escalating profusion is, of course, not perceived as bad news. Quite the opposite, it is precisely what is universally hoped for, sought after, and expected. For many, this is the very definition of *utopia*. It would even be accurate to state that if such profusion *failed* to materialize, we would have billions of bitterly disappointed people.

4. The profusion graph reveals our balance problem.

There are advantages, of course, to such an abundance of profusion. But there are also significant problems. Imbalance, for example. Our modern balance problem is directly related to this graph. When the speed, change, acceleration, and quantities involved are manageable, balance is attainable. But with the speed, change, acceleration, and quantities evident here, imbalance is to be expected. Actually, beyond expected. We can say that under these conditions, imbalance is inevitable.

In addition, as this graph continues to ascend, it will lead to even more speed, change, and instability. Thus our imbalance problems will continue to exacerbate. This does not mean we lay down our guard and acquiesce with a whimper. On the contrary, such a warning means we redouble our vigilance to guard both our balance and our priorities.

In response, we can learn to periodically take segments of our lives off-line, to voluntarily step off the default cultural treadmill from time to time and regain our equilibrium. It is not mandatory to participate in everything progress throws our way.

5. The profusion graph causes increasing stress, and other problems as well.

Imbalance is not the only difficulty represented by this dramatic graph. For example, the verticalization of profusion also results in increasing levels of stress. As if that weren't enough, it also leads to increasing change, complexity, speed, intensity, overload, and volatility.

Each of these issues relates to the matter of human limits. Stress, for example, is not a "bad" thing or a "good" thing. It is value neutral. Having *no stress* in our lives—no change, no challenge, no novelty, no responsibility—is literally fatal. Having only *minimal stress* is boring. But, on the other hand, having *extreme stress* can lead to illness and disability. What we need is the right amount.

God has designed the human body to function best within a range of tolerances, a kind of middle zone. When we understand where the limits are and learn to stay within that range of tolerances, we thrive. This is the benefit of balance—to find and remain in the zone of health, sustainability, productivity, and priorities.

What is true for stress is also true for change, complexity, speed, intensity, and so forth. We invite each of these into our life knowing they serve important purposes. But too much of any becomes toxic. At the appropriate pace of faith and load limit of life, we will live in the center and thrive. But the modern profusion dynamic pushes us, forcefully, in the direction of overload. Always.

6. *The graph also speaks to the balance of good versus evil.*

On two occasions I heard famous Christian leaders asked whether evil had increased in the world today. Both hesitated momentarily and then stated (with the kind of uncertainty that indicted they weren't prepared to bet a cheeseburger on it) that, no, evil had not increased. The implication was that there is no more evil today than a hundred or a thousand years ago. But, clearly, they must be speaking in *qualitative* terms, not *quantitative*. When we bring the issue into the quantitative realm, evil has not only increased, but it has soared alarmingly. The math on this is unanimous.

The profusion curve can be divided into two subcurves—good and evil. Let's grant that good is more abundant than evil by 10:1, or 50:1, or, for the optimists, even 100:1. Nevertheless, both of these subcurves are growing exponentially. In a quantitative sense, therefore, evil is indeed rapidly increasing. And this matches perfectly with the empiric data we see before us.

7. The real force behind this graph is not profusion but progress.

It is now time to become concerned about the power, autonomy, and intentions of progress. If we are to achieve the balance we need, progress must be confronted.

The Power of Progress

Progress has shown a remarkable ability to pile millions of people on its back, even billions, and still go uphill. We should be appropriately thankful for its many gifts. The average modern has literally tens of thousands of reasons to be grateful to progress, and it is only right to express our appreciation on a regular basis.

Yet we are to discern and judge all things, and there is reason for concern. Not only is progress directly responsible for our balance problems (along with our own complicity of course), but it has grown so flush with power and success that it now often operates under an autonomous strength and speed.

Because progress has proven so alluringly proficient, we have decided to build our entire economy around its engines of differentiation, proliferation, combination, invention, and discovery. We hitched our wagon to that star, and progress delivered on a grandiose scale, leaving us both delighted and awed. As a result, our way of life is now predicated upon the growth that progress brings. If progress were to stop or slow, both our economy and our way of life would collapse. And that, of course, will never be allowed to happen.

To continue in the direction we are going—straight up—is our only apparent option. Even if we wanted to stop, slow, or change direction, we would not know how to do so. But it's all a moot point anyway, because who in their right mind wants to stop?

Yet to make our economy completely contingent and dependent on the processes of progress—the processes that always give us more and more of everything faster and faster at exponential rates—might result in something more than our desired prosperity. It might also result in dependence. Indeed, that is our condition today—dependence. Progress is not addicted to us; we are addicted to progress.

If progress leads directly to imbalance—thus placing our priorities at risk—can we ask progress to please be more sensitive? If progress leads to stress and overload, can we appeal for it to slow? It will never happen.

We now live in a different world, a different kind of reality. Yes, progress is biblically normative and thus our friend. God created the world, then created us, then handed us a progress toolbox and said, "Go work on it." His intention was for us to build and create using the tools of progress. But progress lives in a fallen world, a world where nothing is pure, a world where the wheat and the weeds grow in the same field.[4] As a result, progress is not only our friend but also our enemy. We have much wheat, but we also have many weeds. Progress *always* results in more of both.

After studying and reflecting on this for nearly thirty years, I have come to the conclusion that progress—with the economy in tow—is now the most powerful force on the face of the earth. (God excluded, of course.) When you place money and modernity on the same team, well, let's just say there's a certain swagger to the image. Do not underestimate progress. This is not a marshmallow problem; it is a Mt. Everest problem.

Aggressive Progress

I was in Kuwait speaking recently and, at one point, joined an informal discussion about Dubai. Dubai is a modern, affluent city on the Persian Gulf (or, as they prefer to say, the Arabian Gulf) and also one of the seven emirates in the UAE (United Arab Emirates). Although I've never personally visited Dubai, I know many who have vacationed there or transited through their sparkling airport.

At one point in our discussion, a friend mentioned that Dubai has a "very aggressive form of progress." It wasn't intended as a compliment, and I understood instantly what was meant. Yes, I thought—that's the word. They are forcefully pushing for bigger, faster, higher, richer, flashier. On the one hand, it's quite impressive to find man-made islands shaped like palm trees that can be seen from space; or a hotel shaped like a giant sail (the Burj) that is the world's tallest, most luxurious, and only seven-star hotel; or the world's largest indoor skiing facility. But that's not all. In various stages of construction or planning (and each hampered by the 2007–2010 global economic recession), the city is pursuing construction of:

- The world's first completely underwater hotel
- The World Islands, a complex of 300 artificially created islands in the shape of the world
- The world's tallest building
- The world's largest amusement park, twice the size and capacity of Disney World in Orlando
- The world's largest shopping mall, with over nine million square feet of shopping
- The world's first spaceport

I don't mean to single out Dubai; there are innumerable examples of epic ostentatious architectural egotism across the globe, many in the United States (Las Vegas and Atlantic City come to mind). But it was the term *aggressive progress* that caught my attention.

When progress functions as a servant to the legitimate needs of humanity, it has no equal. Serving righteous purposes, it has delivered billions of people from conditions of deprivation and ignorance and brought opportunity, education, healing, and prosperity around the globe at levels unimagined in human history.

But when progress becomes aggressive—in concert with evil, greedy, egotistical, maniacal human intentions—it must be called out. If it charges too fast and too high and too quickly without regard for limits or wisdom or humanity, then it will cause problems unparalleled in history.

CHAPTER

3

HOW BALANCE IS DISPLAYED IN EVERY QUADRANT OF THE CREATED ORDER

MOE WAS BORN to a strict poor family in Kitchener, Ontario. He used bobby pins to hold up his pants and tape to hold his shoes together. At age six, he was struck by a car in a tragic accident, resulting in frontal lobe brain damage. His entire life people regarded him as strange, different, weird, eccentric. He was a shy social misfit and had a grand total of three dates. He never owned a telephone. He wore clashing clothes, always wrinkled. He talked rapidly in clipped, repeated phrases with a singsong cadence. He got traffic citations for driving too slowly, lived out of his car for parts of his life, and forever had trouble managing money.

But Moe Norman was also a genius and perhaps the best golfer who ever lived. He had a photographic memory, often reciting facts for those interested: that he'd played 434 different golf courses, remembered the exact yardage and layout for virtually every golf hole he'd ever walked, and once hit exactly 2,207 balls in a day. He could calculate mathematical equations with lightning speed and was unbeatable at cards.

Professional golfing in Canada paid little money in the 1950s, so Moe resorted to sleeping in sand bunkers and hitchhiking around. He set bowling pins in the winter to earn enough to play the links in the summer. He would use the same ball continuously until it wore out, then search for another in the bushes.

He won fifty-seven tournaments, set forty course records, and had seventeen holes-in-one. He could hit a ball a hundred times off the tee and not disturb the peg—not even one millimeter. "I hit balls," he said, "not tees." In tournaments, he would entertain crowds by hitting off the mouth of a coke bottle. He played extremely fast, not even slowing to line up putts.

Sam Snead once called Norman the greatest striker of the ball. The two were playing an exhibition when both needed about 250 yards to clear the stream. Snead "laid up," stroking his ball short of the creek, and then watched Norman prepare to go for it. "You need to lay up, Moe," said Snead, "you can't carry that creek." Norman replied, "I'm aiming for the bridge." His shot rolled directly across the bridge, and Snead never again attempted to give advice. In the 1950s, Ben Hogan and Norman were hitting practice shots together when Hogan asserted there was no such thing as an intentionally straight golf shot. Moe proceeded to hit one straight shot after another, causing Hogan to mutter about how he "kept hitting those accidents." Palmer, Player, and Nicklaus all marveled at his ability.

"I don't know of any player, ever, who could strike a golf ball like Moe Norman," said Lee Trevino, "as far as hitting it solid, knowing where it is going and knowing what he wants to do with the ball. Moe Norman is a genius when it comes to playing the game of golf." Fred Couples once asked him in jest, "Have you ever actually mis-hit a ball?" Moe confessed, "Yes, in 1962." VJ Singh was asked who was the best golfer he'd ever seen. "Moe Norman. I've hit balls with him lots of times. He was incredible. Whatever he said he could do, he could do. If you talk to Lee Trevino and the other greats of the game, they'll tell you how good he was. He could talk it, and he could do it. God gives people little gifts, and Moe had a gift for golf."

"I don't go to church, but I certainly pray a lot," Moe said. "Always have. One of my sisters was a nun, and when I was young my parents dragged me to church by the seat of my pants. God is real—He has to be, because no man could develop the talent I have on his own. I am the world's best ball striker and teacher because it was His will. Why did He choose me to be the best who ever lived? I don't have the faintest idea. That's why there's a hereafter—so one day I can find out."[1]

Golf has been called the most difficult game on the planet, a hopeless endeavor, a boulevard of broken dreams, an exercise in masochism, the cruelest game, an awkward set of bodily contortions, and an endless series of tragedies. I once watched a doctor slice two consecutive balls into the pond off the first hole. He stormed over to the water, threw his clubs in with a violent splash, and walked away. This physician was both highly intelligent and exceptionally athletic—but the game beat him in five minutes. Moe Norman—neither intelligent nor athletic—could hit 200,000 balls without missing the fairway.

It appears to me that Moe had an unusual form of savant syndrome. Savants are people with very narrow islands of intelligence that are also very deep. They often have significant neurological limitations such as mental retardation, cerebral palsy, autism, blindness, or deafness. But, in contrast, they have remarkable neurologic giftedness and exceptional abilities: lightning calculators, astounding musical gifts, artistry, speed reading, prodigious memories.

In Moe's case, it seems that the deep intelligence had something to do with neuromuscular memory. "The game of golf is played at the limits of the ability of the nervous system to reproducibly make precise, ballistic movements," explains Dr. John Milton, Professor of Neuroscience. Consider that the motion of lifting a spoonful of food to the mouth involves the use of more than thirty joints in the shoulder, arm, wrist, and fingers. A golf swing exceeds this complexity by countless orders of magnitude. "Pre-programming of the motor cortex for voluntary movements" is followed by the "kinematic sequence for the swing"—a sequential transfer of power from legs to hips to pelvis to back to shoulders to arm to shot.[2] Nearly every muscle along this route is employed, each firing with precise timing, in proper sequence, and to the appropriate extent. A golfer employs vision, depth perception, proprioception, coordination, timing, power, strength, speed, and, yes, balance. Everything must come together simultaneously and accurately for the shot to work.

Feel free to challenge me if you wish, but I agree with Moe Norman's assessment. It was God who placed within him the precise balance of all the necessary elements to strike the ball perfectly a hundred thousand times in a row, "because no man could develop the talent I have on his own." This is, I believe, a sign to us. The same magnificence of balance and precision, so improbably accomplished in Moe's physiology, is similarly—and even more improbably—spread across the entire cosmos. We are surrounded, continuously, by balance. From the quantum dimensions of subatomic particles to the galactic expanse of the entire universe, God has placed on display the design requirement of balance.

If balance has been thus ordained throughout all the created order, isn't this an indication for us to similarly respect balance in our personal lives? God is speaking not *disorder* to us, but *order*: Find the center, and rest in it.

Crowned with Glory and Honor — and Balance

Before launching into the stars in search of balance, let's first look in the mirror to see what we might discover. Staring back at us—despite our protestations—is the pinnacle of God's creative genius. There exists no evidence whatever that anything as densely organized or complex as the human body will ever be found elsewhere in the universe.

Actually, it would be accurate to say that the human body is itself a universe. Made up of 10^{28} atoms (1 followed by 28 zeros), we each contain millions of times more atoms than there are stars in space ($\sim 10^{22}$). Ninety percent of these atoms are replaced every year, and virtually 100 percent are replaced every five years. Thus our physical beings are continuously tearing down but also continuously building up. From dust we come and to dust we return—continuously.

The human brain has one hundred billion neurons, the basic cell of the nervous system. Each neuron is connected to dendrites and axons. If all our nervous tissue were stretched end to end, it would extend for more than one hundred thousand miles. The three-pound brain is capable of holding the equivalent of twenty-five million books, more than all the volumes in the Library of Congress. Its computational power is ten thousand trillion computations per second, exceeding the fastest supercomputers.

The ear has a million moving parts and can hear over a range of sound intensities that vary by a factor of one trillion. The sound wave has almost no energy associated with it—a person could talk for a lifetime and not generate enough energy to boil a cup of water. We hear *only* because of the extreme sensitivity of the hearing mechanism.

The heart beats two and a half billion times in a lifetime and pumps blood over sixty thousand miles of blood vessels. Our smallest capillaries are so delicate that the vessel wall can be torn with 1/3000th the tension required to tear tissue paper. We make two million red blood cells every second. If all our red blood cells were taken out of our body and placed end to end, they would circle the earth at the equator four times.

The body has one hundred trillion cells, each with a nucleus. Inside the nucleus are twenty-three pairs of chromosomes containing approximately 24,000 genes, referred to as the Human Genome. All of this is constructed with DNA and contains the hard-wiring for much of our physiology and psychology. If we extracted the DNA from all one hundred trillion cells and compacted it together, it would fit inside a golf ball. But, if, instead, we superglued the ends together, it would reach one hundred billion miles long.

We each began life as a single cell, fertilized while sashaying through our mother's fallopian tube. Our initial single-cell DNA—that God used to grow each of us—weighed two-tenths of a millionth of a millionth of an ounce. If we collected the initial single-cell DNA from every human being alive on the earth today and placed it on a scale, it would weigh 1/1000th of an ounce.[3]

Perhaps it is possible to yawn through this and fail to be impressed by the unparalleled sophistication residing inside our own skin—but we'd have to be in a coma. Undeniably, we are factories that never shut down, each made up of trillions upon trillions of working units, all perpetually moving, metabolizing, combining, interacting, adjusting, purifying, purging, building, and decaying. Yet everything functions in *balance.* If this balance is disturbed, disease results.

When organ systems are functioning in a balanced manner, physicians say they are "compensated." To be decompensated, i.e., out of balance, is to be ill. Likewise, in the area of mental health, when someone is functioning poorly it is said he or she is "unbalanced." For physiology to avoid becoming pathology, balance is essential. It is no different in the broader context of life.

Homeostasis

As it turns out, the human body is very good at this balancing act. One of the most fiercely defended guardians of human physiology is called homeostasis (Greek: "staying the same"). This is the ability of the body to stay in the middle, to fight for equilibrium. It does not mean that all change is disallowed, but only that any change is incorporated into the norm as quickly as possible and then equilibrium is reestablished.

The body uses multiple feedback systems, both positive and negative, to assure homeostasis. As explained by Yale surgeon Sherwin B. Nuland, MD, in his book *How We Live,*

> They come into play as part of the body's constant readjustments intended to support living processes by maintaining internal equilibrium . . . The maintenance of the body's homeostasis requires the integrated coordination of every tissue within it . . . It is homeostasis, the dependability and steadiness of the internal environment, that keeps us alive.[4]

When this process fails, the results are painful. First, our bodies begin to function suboptimally. Then we become ill. And, if left uncorrected, we often die. Because the body has such a powerful drive to survive, and because homeostasis is an important custodian of that drive, the entire body is charged with monitoring and protecting this gift of equilibrium. "There can be no chemical complacency," writes Dr. Nuland.

> If an organism is to survive, every activity within it must in some way be part of the effort. Moreover, it is imperative that there be

total coordination if the outcome is to be the singular momentum that is ongoing life. The integration of all parts of this effort has a seeming wisdom about it, by which the multiplicity of processes is somehow guided into a harmonious whole. The essence of success is the dynamism that allows each cell to respond instantaneously to even the most minor threat to its integrity and therefore to the integrity of the entire organism . . . A high degree of radical readiness . . . is required to allow the immediate change that corrects a tendency toward imbalance.[5]

It would seem logical for us to take a lesson from our bodies—remembering that they represent God's most glorious creation this side of heaven—and develop a personal appreciation for homeostasis in the larger context of life. Perhaps we too should employ positive and negative feedback systems to alert us so that, once alerted, we could return to the safety of equilibrium.

Movement, Coordination, and Balance

Homeostasis is of incalculable worth to our internal physiological equilibrium, but, in addition, the body has other balancing skills. Many of us feel perhaps quite unathletic, and don't expect the Bolshoi Ballet or the U.S. Gymnastics Team to come knocking on our door anytime soon. Grace is the last word we expect to hear applied to our stumbling movements. Still, we *did* take those first steps, not a small accomplishment considering we only used two feet—not four—and had to conquer gravity with our tiny cerebellum.

Routine daily activities, such as reaching for a pencil or tying our shoes, require a remarkably complex effort of movement, coordination, and balance. "Most of our brain is geared toward action," states neurologist Apostolos P. Georgopoulos at the University of Minnesota. Vast areas of our central nervous system "are intimately connected and cooperate in initiating, producing, and controlling coordinating movements and maintaining body balance."[6]

Even if we personally are not prime examples of gymnastic artistry, still we can watch with appreciation when the human body floats through the air like Michael Jordan, or vaults, flips, and twists before landing on one foot like Kari Shrug (my favorite Olympic moment), or walks the high wire like Kurt Wallenda. "Humans possess a phenomenal ability to roll, twist, spin, jump, twirl, flip, run, leap, and lunge, as a single motion or in complex combinations, in bare feet or with slippers, shoes, skates, skis, boards, or rollers, forwards or backwards, on one leg or with two, or simply to balance motionless on one arm or tiptoe on the top of a champagne bottle," says physician/engineer Randy J. Guliuzza, MD.

> Ballerinas, gymnasts, and ice skaters depend on their bodies' ability to not only balance, but also to sense speed of rotation and body position, and then make just the right body adjustments. How does all of this work together? It is clear that there is no such thing as an isolated "balance system." The body uses all of its systems to balance and, in the process, ingeniously exploits properties of nature such as inertia, momentum, and gravity. In this area, humans are unmatched.[7]

No matter where we personally find ourselves on the graceful-awkward spectrum, it is easy to recognize that bodily movement under the influence of coordination and balance is a gift to be cherished. But it is foolish in the extreme for us to tempt disaster in an Evel Knievel-like fashion, unless we don't mind endless concussions and thirty-seven broken bones. Once again, we find that balance is a gift, outside the bounds of which lurks disaster.

Vestibular System

The final balancing system of the body is located in the inner ear. The bizarre-looking vestibular apparatus is the only organ dedicated exclusively to balance functions. Even at twenty-weeks gestation, it is helping the baby determine balance in the uterus, a skill that later contributes to a head-down position for birth. The tiny otolithic organs are responsible for the perception of linear acceleration, while the three semicircular canals sense rotational movement. For this purpose they are positioned at right angles to each other. When the head rotates, fluid shifts in the canals. This excites tiny hair cells that transfer mechanical movement into electrical impulses. This information is then communicated to the brain.

We marvel at the sophistication of this tiny system and are grateful when it works as designed. Any malfunction can be not only disorienting but also literally nauseating—and dangerous. The tragic death of John F. Kennedy Jr., his wife, Carolyn Bessette, and her sister, Lauren Bessette, revealed, once again, why we ought not tempt the limits of equilibrium. All experienced pilots understand that those lacking instrument rating must not fly beyond the orienting capacity of their vestibular system. Kennedy challenged this wisdom and lost. Experiencing spatial disorientation over water with poor visibility, he crashed into the Atlantic Ocean on his way to Martha's Vineyard.

Perhaps we too should learn to take care when disoriented. Perhaps we are moving too fast and flying beyond the specifications of our internal balancing equipment, disregarding the signs that danger lurks. And, of course, it is not only ourselves who face the consequences but also those near us, those we love the most. People are drawn to the name of Kennedy because of its fame and perhaps the indelible image of little John-John saluting his father's passing funeral carriage. But we overlook that the Bessette family, too, paid the ultimate price, twice over. I was not surprised to hear that a wrongful-death case was settled out of court for a reported $50 million.

/ / / /

The record God has written in the human body is, first of all, that it is spectacular and complex beyond human comprehension—no physician will ever understand it. And second, that balance is commended as normative, the position of health, safety, and sustainability. Dr. Nuland repeatedly speaks to this theme using not only the terms *balance* and *homeostasis* but also *equilibrating steadiness, constancy, order, integrated coordination, stability, sustained harmony,* and *consistency,* and then summarizes by saying, "Whatever else it may be, life is one big balancing act."[8]

It is, for us, a sign . . .

The Precision and Balance of a Life-Permitting Universe

The human body provides remarkable evidence of nature's balance principle, but there is more to our case. Explorers ranging far and wide across the celestial expanse will uncover both precision and balance everywhere they look—small and large, familiar and strange, fast and slow, light and dark, matter and antimatter, stars, galaxies, and supernovas, the laws of physics, chemistry, and biology, the four fundamental forces, mathematics, and singularities.

Let's begin with the most familiar, our blue-green planet Earth. To some, our small globe seems cosmically insignificant, a random traveler in space hitchhiking alongside a mediocre star, itself an accidental piece of celestial dust stuck to the Milky Way pinwheel, spinning wildly around a black hole with no idea of the direction of its path or the purpose of its journey, awaiting annihilation at the hands of an asteroid the size of Delaware.

But that is not the majority opinion, not God's opinion, not what the evidence says, and not the truth. The magnificence of our campground is "a glimpse of divinity," observed one astronaut from space. "Earth's crammed with heaven," wrote Elizabeth Barrett Browning, "And every common bush afire with God." "There was a time when meadow, grove and stream, The earth and every common sight, To me did seem appareled in celestial light," exclaimed Wordsworth. "Earth laughs in flowers," added Emerson. We pitch our tent on top of an enormous painting and drive our stakes into trembling earth, for it is an energetic planet. "When we contemplate the whole globe as one great dewdrop, striped and dotted with continents and islands, flying through space with other stars all singing and shining together as one, the whole universe appears as an infinite storm of beauty," wrote John Muir.

This is more than just poetic sentimentality. Before our beloved planet could be life-permitting and inhabited by humans, an impossibly narrow set of specifications needed to be met. Prior to Earth welcoming complex life, the bubble first had to be balanced precisely on the center line at both the subatomic and galactic levels.

Earth is just the right distance from the sun, inside the circumstellar habitable zone, and the sun is just the right kind of star—not too hot, not too cold. Our relationship with the sun is completely one-sided: It gives, and we take. Of course, the sun has an almost inexhaustible energy supply from which to draw. As a nonstop thermonuclear bomb, every second it converts five million tons of mass to energy and then shoots the photons in all directions. After traveling eight minutes, we intercept one-billionth of this total solar energy output and yet that suffices for virtually all our needs. It is just the right amount. If we received twice that many photons, we would cook, or half that many, we would freeze. A pinhead-sized spot on Earth is struck by one trillion photons per second, bringing to mind physicist James Jeans' observation that "the Great Architect of the Universe now begins to appear as a pure mathematician."[9]

Earth also has just the right kind and size of moon. If our large moon did not exist, neither would we. Our friendly parish lantern has a diameter almost one-fourth that of Earth. This size stabilizes the angle of our axis of spin. Were it not for the moon, Earth's obliquity (tilt of its axis) would vary chaotically from 0 to 85 degrees[10] and would be catastrophically influenced by Jupiter's gravitational pull.[11] As a result, the stability of our climate is to a large extent the result of the existence of the moon. Without the moon's benediction, Earth would rotate three times faster, subjecting us to continuous gale force winds.

Earth has a crust just thick enough to maintain plate-tectonic activity, a phenomenon also known as continental drift. A solid inner metallic core is surrounded by a molten metallic outer core and then overlaid with the mantle. The mantle, or crust, is not a continuous structure but instead individual plates that fit together like a jigsaw puzzle. Earth, as far as we know, is the only planet in our solar system to exhibit plate tectonics. This provides for biodiversity, stabilizes temperature and climate, and guarantees the separation of sea and land.

Earth has the required strong magnetic field, thanks to three factors: plate tectonics, a liquid conducting core of iron-nickel, and a rapid spinning rate (once every 23.93 hours). This magnetic field shields us from dangerous incoming cosmic radiation and deflects most of the sun's charged atomic particles around the earth. The aurora borealis is glorious evidence of this deflection for those fortunate enough to witness it.

Earth is in the right kind of solar system with giant planets that shield the inner planets from too many impacts from comets or asteroids. Jupiter's mass, for example, is 317 times that of Earth, and Saturn's is 95 times.[12] These huge outer planets, especially Jupiter, function as oversized planetary offensive linemen blocking intruding errant cosmic bodies out of Earth's orbital path.

In *Rare Earth*, two University of Washington scientists, geologist Peter Ward and astronomer Donald Brownlee, speak to the precise requirements met by our planet for life. "It appears that we have been quite lucky," they write, explaining how the development of life on our hospitable planet required a "fortuitous assemblage of the correct elements" and "an intricate set of nearly irreproducible circumstances."[13]

"If some god-like being could be given the opportunity to plan a sequence of events with the express goal of duplicating our 'Garden of Eden,' that power would face a formidable task. With the best intentions, but limited by natural laws and materials, it is unlikely that Earth could ever be truly replicated. Too many processes in its formation involved sheer luck." Their conclusion: "It appears that Earth got it just right."[14] Due to the statistical improbability, it is their belief that no matter how hard we search for another life-sustaining planet, we will come up empty. The math points in the direction of uniqueness.

As we lift our examination beyond the borders of our own planet, we find abundant additional evidence that balance and precision were involved in setting up a life-gifting universe. Regardless which theory of cosmology is involved, there is universal consensus that the odds were astronomical against a successful universe-galaxy-solar system-earth-life spectrum happening.

As noted physicist and cosmologist Paul Davies, winner of the

Templeton Award and Britain's Faraday prize, explains in *Cosmic Jackpot: Why Our Universe Is Just Right for Life*, if the laws of physics varied even slightly from their exact values, then life would not be possible. This has been called the "Goldilocks 'Just Right' Effect." Everything must be precisely fine-tuned—yet there is no scientific reason why, in fact, everything is indeed tuned with such astounding precision. The balance simply exists, and, say the scientists, it is duly noted.

The number of stars in the universe needs to be just what it is. There need to be three spatial dimensions rather than two or four. The weak nuclear force needs to be just what is it. The strong nuclear force has to be just what it is. The electromagnetic force has to be exactly what it is. The gravitational force needs to be precisely as it is. The ratio between the electromagnetic force and the gravitational force needs to be exactly what it is. The number of electrons compared to protons needs to be just what it is. The mass of the neutron needs to be precisely as it is.

In order for carbon to exist, the nuclear resonance needs to be at just the right energy for helium and beryllium to combine—and, yes, it turns out to be precisely that energy. Just because the nuclear resonance *needs* to be this precise level does not mean there is any scientific reason *why it is indeed this level*. Since all of life is carbon-based, from a scientific perspective, all of life is a statistical fluke.

Davies saves his largest exclamations for dark energy. The story of dark energy is extreme in this regard, to the point that he calls it the biggest fix in the universe. Dark energy, according to Davies, is perhaps the most dangerous stuff known to science. The universe is filled with it—in fact, 74 percent of the mass-energy of the entire cosmos is dark energy—but we don't know what it is. We do, however, know some things about its precision. The amount and characteristics of dark energy need to exist at such a precise level that "*life is balanced on a knife-edge* is a staggering understatement in this case: no knife in the universe could have an edge that fine."[15]

Using the metaphor of a Designer Machine, Davies suggests that "the collection of felicitous 'coincidences' in physics and cosmology implies that the Great Designer had better set knobs carefully, or the universe would be a very inhospitable place."[16]

Imagine playing the role of an intelligent designer, planning a universe fit for life. The present universe works well enough, but how much could you change without spoiling things? It's possible that you could do away with some sorts of galaxy or eliminate giant black holes. Some small stars and large planets might be superfluous. At the atomic level, you could probably get rid of a few elements, but most are needed somewhere in the life story. At a more fundamental level, you would be wise to leave things completely alone. Getting rid of electrons would be a disaster, as chemistry would then be impossible. Abolishing neutrons would rule out any element other than hydrogen. The inventory of fundamental particles is not a good place to tinker. Even meddling with the properties of these particles would be risky.

Given the necessity of keeping things pretty much as they are, the question arises of why the universe consists of the things that it does. Why are there electrons, protons, neutrons, and all the other atomic components? Why do these entities have the properties that they do? Why do the particles all have particular masses and electric charges, and not others?[17]

"The chances that the universe should be life-permitting are so infinitesimal as to be incomprehensible and incalculable," says philosopher William Craig Lane. "Improbability is multiplied by improbability until our minds are reeling in incomprehensible numbers. There is no physical reason why these constants and quantities should possess the values they do."[18] If almost any of the basic features of the universe were different, life would not be possible. It is a bit like winning the mega-lottery of the galaxy by stumbling over a pebble in a darkened parking lot and having the billion-dollar winning ticket—just blown out the window of a passing eighteen-wheeler from Houston—stick to the end of your nose.

"The universe appears to have been incredibly 'fine-tuned' for our existence," continues Lane. "In the various fields of physics and astrophysics, classical cosmology, quantum mechanics, and biochemistry, discoveries have repeatedly disclosed that intelligent carbon-based life on

Earth requires a delicate balance of physical and cosmological quantities. If any one of these quantities were slightly altered, the balance would be destroyed, and life would not exist."[19]

We have the privilege of living in a time when the balance principle has now been thoroughly researched and found to be a dominant presence not only in physics and cosmology, but in nearly every avenue of investigation. In population demographics, for example, the number of births must balance the population loss to keep at least a stable level—even though today many countries are falling dangerously below this level and committing demographic suicide. In economics, we are always preaching (if seldom achieving) a personal balance between spending and savings, a governmental balanced budget, and a stable international balance of payments. Thus, whether in the social sciences, political sciences, biological sciences, physical sciences, or mathematics we discover the same message, that balance plays a naturally dominant role.

Yes, we do indeed find exceptions to this, times when imbalance and disequilibrium are not only appropriate but desired—times of growth and improvement, training and testing, expansion, experimentation, and exploration. Recognizing their importance, I not only fully endorse these times but also participate in them. To enter marathon training, climb a mountain, go on a fast, participate in an intensive study program, adopt a child, accept the presidency of a service organization, write a book, move to a different house—each of these can induce an appropriate state of disequilibrium. As long as these occasions do not disrupt our core priorities, I find no fault with them, and the natural order is replete with millions of additional illustrations.

But after the departure, we either *return to equilibrium* or else *establish a new level of equilibrium*. That is the message of the universe.

HOW TO PLACE YOUR LIFE IN STABLE ORBIT AROUND YOUR PRIORITIES

I HAVE SEEN many people die. Most physicians have, at least those working the front lines. It is a jarring experience, even on the hundredth occasion. Being in the room at such times is an event like none other. Nothing in medicine compares, nor in all of life. Something irreversible changes in the world. A person who was here is no longer here.

Sometimes relatives are present when it happens—perhaps a patient on the ward has been slipping for days and the entire family is now assembled bedside. At other times, perhaps a Code Blue in the ER, the relatives are not permitted in attendance and are instead waiting down the hall in the family room. They realize that solemn professionals are working furiously and that mortality hangs by a thread. The images looping around their brains are like personal horror films played at triple speed.

To be candid, it is an enormous privilege to be in the room when someone passes into the next life. It is a deeply spiritual moment, and one almost feels the urge to take off one's shoes for it is holy ground. It is also a weighty privilege to tell the family. When the patient succumbs and the heroism is called off, someone needs to inform them. It's simultaneously the worst job in the world and a high honor. It calls for sensitivity, compassion, and patience. Lots of patience. If you are in a hurry, it's best to send someone else.

Some people die quickly. In these cases, I'm always impressed by how fragile life is. I remember well the case of an elderly man and his wife of sixty years. They were eating dinner at home when she complained of chest pain. They got into the car, and the husband headed off toward the Emergency Room. When her pain increased, he went faster, glancing worriedly at the road, then his wife, then the road again. His eyesight wasn't good, nor his reflexes, and he just couldn't bring himself to career through residential streets. It was comforting when the hospital came into view—but then she clutched her chest and began to perspire. He drove faster. In another minute he'd reach the intersection in front of the hospital, then a right turn would bring him into the emergency entrance. But it was Friday evening and the traffic was congested. As he approached the corner, the light turned red. He was three cars back and boxed in. He fidgeted and looked at his wife and held her hand. Then she let out a moan and died. Right there, stuck at the red light, one hundred yards from the ER, she departed this world and flew to her next destination. By the time they brought her in on a stretcher, there was nothing we could do. She had lived eighty-two fairly healthy years, but in fifteen brief minutes and without any warning, it was over.

Other people die slowly. Some very, very slowly. In these cases, I'm impressed not with how fragile life is, but how resilient it can be. These hardy folk survive heart attacks, cancer, diabetes, cigarettes, alcohol, inactivity, bronchitis, congestive heart failure, renal insufficiency, swollen extremities, and obesity, but still, inexplicably, they hang on. When the final downhill slide begins, it can be very tentative, almost dawdling. This can make the vigil awkward. Families ask "how long?" but it is best never to venture a guess. After weeks of waiting, finally the day arrives. The patient descends gradually into unconsciousness. The breathing slows, and any discernable pulse is lost. Next, the nurse can't find the blood pressure. The monitor EKG shows a slowing blip, then slower, then erratic. You understand what is happening—everyone does—that this is not reversible, that this patient is dead. But not yet. The body lies very still. Suddenly, a gurgling noise shocks the room. Then, thirty seconds later, a slight gasp. You wait. In some cases, the monitor is removed so random spikes don't confuse everyone. Still, you wait. You don't want to pronounce death and then have a twitch.

However it happens, there is one gift that death always grants those surviving—the gift of knowing for sure, even if for a very short time, what matters most. For that brief span of time, the world stops. Our focus is arrested. Death, as nothing else, commands our full attention.

The Things That Matter Most

There are things in life that matter a little, and there are things in life that matter a lot. But I am primarily interested in the things that matter most. I like to believe that we are all interested in these—the highest motives we aspire to, the noblest impulses of existence, the pinnacle values that deserve their place on the mountaintop where we can always see them and be guided by them. I am speaking of the timeless, the unchanging, the eternal.

Hopefully these priorities are identified early in life—often handed down generationally—and always looked upon with a firm sense of commitment. We learn that our Creator is a personal God full of love and grace, that truth exists and is knowable, that there is a difference between right and wrong, that genuineness and uprightness are universally respected, that givers are more joyous than takers, that it is fine to have money but even better to have integrity. And, hopefully, we grow to understand that people are more important than things and that love matters more than all the houses, cars, and boats in the universe added together and multiplied times infinity.

I am neither naïve nor unrealistic. It's nice to talk high-mindedness, but meanwhile, practically speaking, we need to put in the hours at work and feed the family while making sure the seat belts are secured and the dental appointments remembered. And that's before we factor in the trivial and the mundane because we've also got to vacuum the car, mow the lawn, paint the deck, clean the closets, deworm the dog, check the email, and watch our three and a half hours of daily TV. At some level, this kind of cultural clutter is unavoidable and, we might even say, not always inappropriate. Personally

I love to mow my lawn and work around the house. But the point is, *none of this will matter on that final day.* The gift of our deathbed is that everything else disappears, swept away by the forceful purity of culmination. The only things left standing are those that matter most.

One year after receiving a diagnosis of pancreatic cancer, Apple Computer founder Steve Jobs stood before Stanford University's graduating class to reflect on his deathbed.

> Remembering that I'll be dead soon is the most important thing I've ever encountered to help me make the big choices in life, because almost everything—all external expectations, all pride, all fear of embarrassment or failure—these things just fall away in the face of death, leaving only what is truly important. Remembering that you are going to die is the best way I know to avoid the trap of thinking you have something to lose. You are already naked.[1]

If this sounds morbid, I would beg you to reconsider. To refuse contemplation of our dying deprives us of the best corrective to our living. The last days of our lives will silence petty activities and superficial appetites and replace them with a unique clarity of focus. I have learned such lessons from patients who have died under my care, and also from their families and friends. In each instance, it has been my privilege to place myself intentionally and willingly on that bed and to invite that moment to be my teacher.

Some of these people have been ready. They have anticipated the occasion for years, and now that it is upon them, they are neither surprised nor anxious. They do not fear stepping across the threshold from earth to eternity. They do not need to spend this last day in apology but rather in misty-eyed gratitude and affectionate goodbyes. Nothing in all of human existence compares to the anguished joy of this experience.

Others are ill-prepared, disillusioned, and alone. They lived life "my way," as the song says, following their instincts, enjoying their freedoms, pursuing their hormones, enlarging their barns, and piling up mountains of booty. But they were inattentive to this final bed because it was never part of their calculus.

When the sand finally vanishes from our hourglass, the spotlight will be on our priorities. Did we choose them wisely and hold to them resolutely? Will this be our eulogy? Or were we casual in following the crowd and, in the end, never took seriously the things that mattered most?

Finding Stable Orbit Around Our Priorities

Balance does not exist for balance's sake. It does not exist to crown itself king and control our lives with an intimidating set of rules. It does not exist to make us feel guilty, frustrated, and defeated. It exists to serve us. It exists, largely, as a tool in service of our priorities.

Yes, of course, balance is also a major contributor to sustainability, just as it contributes to focus, renewal, energy, rest, productivity, and margin. But, in the end, each of these is only a tool. Valuable tools, to be sure—but in the end, only tools.

Why, then, are we placing so much emphasis on balance if it is only a tool? Because it serves such a vital role in guarding our priorities. Tools are important, but priorities are all-important. Tools assist us in living, but priorities are the essence of living. If we neglect our tools, we can be forgiven. But if we neglect our priorities, we will have eternal regrets.

Given the importance of priorities against the widespread disequilibrium of our age, balance is not only an invaluable tool but an increasingly indispensable one. Priorities are under assault, and without a sense of balance, they will blur and drift out of sight. People without balance live a multitasking ricochet life blown by the winds of the world and the trends of the culture.

Once we understand and embrace the relationship between balance and priorities, then we are ready to place

our priorities at the center of our existence
and
our lives in balanced orbit about these priorities.

Placing our lives in a stable, balanced orbit around our core priorities is the first step in achieving a balanced life. More instruction is needed before we can claim victory, but without this first step, we will likely float, rudderless and anchorless.

The idea of our lives orbiting our priorities is helpful because it is visual, functional, and anchoring.

The *visual* aspect comes into play because of the clarity and simplicity of the picture this forms. Our core priorities occupy the center, and our lives orbit around these central priorities. No matter where we are in the orbit, our priorities are always in sight, and we are always in contact with the core. In a sense, it is as if our priorities act as our sun, giving us light and energy. When we speak of centering our lives, it is with reference to this set of core priorities.

The *functional* aspect of this description comes because an orbiting body can travel in different directions and at different speeds, but always in relation to the center. The earth, for example, orbits the sun. But every six months, it is actually heading in the *opposite* direction than it was half a year earlier. In addition, the earth's orbit is not a pure circle but is three million miles farther from the sun in July than it is in January. When it is closest to the sun, it speeds up. When it is farthest, it slows. Thus even though our lives might be changing speed, direction, and nearness relative to our priorities, nevertheless we remain in orbit around core priorities that themselves are durable.

The *anchoring* aspect of this model comes when we realize that the orbiting bodies in a planetary system are never the center of gravity—that distinction always belongs to the star in the middle. In the case of our solar system, 99.86 percent of the total mass is contained in the sun. Similarly, as long as our priorities are chosen wisely, they have the power to keep us centered by virtue of their inherent substantiality, as in the Russian proverb, "One word of truth outweighs the world."

What is the center of gravity of our lives? Does it anchor us reliably against the storms of life? Will we remain tethered to the things that matter most? These are the questions our deathbed is asking us.

Flexibility and Variability

To extend the analogy further, consider the difference between our planet and Pluto. Earth's orbit is nearly a circle, but Pluto's is very elliptical. At the peak of its aphelion, it is almost twice as far from the sun as at its perihelion—a difference of two billion miles.[2] Another difference: Earth's orbit lies in a horizontal plane with regard to the other planets, but the orbit of Pluto (no longer classified a planet) shoots off in a tangent seventeen degrees at variance from the rest. Initial impressions would suggest Earth and Pluto have little in common, but, in fact, they both circle the same center. In this sense, the shape of my orbit might vary dramatically from yours even though we are united in sharing the same core priorities.

This reality—that Earth and Pluto appear very dissimilar yet share the same center—leads to an examination of several misconceptions about balance.

1. The balance principle does not require **uniformity**.

Uniformity implies that everyone does the same things and believes the same things and shares the same traditions in the same way. In reality, the observed variability from person to person is not something to kick against, for it is a freedom given us by God. We have different ages, different genders, different interests, different talents, different backgrounds, different educations, different ethnicities, different experiences, different gifts, different DNA—and we each also have different orbits. *Every person on the planet has a unique orbit.* It is easy for me to accept the will of the Father in this matter, for if the whole world were a clone of me, even I wouldn't want to live there.

Forced uniformity only yields the opposite of uniformity, when people inevitably rebel and flee in different directions. It is important to point out, however, that *uniformity* and *unity* are different entities. While enforced uniformity is impossible, unity is not only possible but precious. Mercury does not need an "extreme makeover" to become like Jupiter. They both circle the same sun, both belong to the same team, both play their unique roles, and both can celebrate their unity in diversity.

2. The balance principle does not require **legalism**.

Legalism implies a set of rules applied to everyone that must never be broken. One of the frustrations expressed by those who try to implement balance but quit in frustration is they "can't keep all the rules." Setting up a rigid structure might work for some but will result in exasperation for most. If we try to exercise every morning from 6:00 to 6:25, then shower and dress from 6:25 to 6:50, then read the Bible and pray from 6:50 to 7:10, then eat breakfast with the family from 7:10 to 7:53, then get in the car at 7:53, then . . .

Some people might prefer this approach, and it can work well for certain personalities and relational structures. But that does not mean it can be generalized to include everyone. For most, life simply contains too many variables, and flexibility is helpful.

3. The balance principle does not require **rigid mathematics**.

This approach reduces everything to a spreadsheet and then forces our lives to artificially fit preset mathematical expectations on a daily or weekly basis. Some decide they will spend forty hours per week at work (not more, not less), two hours per week dating their spouses, ten hours per week interacting with the children, three hours per week exercising, fifty hours per week sleeping, and so on. While structures can be useful in defending boundaries, a rigid spreadsheet will usually cause undo anxiety and unnecessary guilt.

As already discussed, today's world is wild and unruly—a bit like a nonstop rodeo featuring only wild bronc riding. For the majority of us, rigid mathematics will break down in the face of such a pounding environment. A degree of day-to-day, week-to-week, and even month-to-month variability is required to accommodate the uneven pressures we face.

/ / / /

Having taken such pains to differentiate balance from rigidity does not mean all structure is invalid. *Of course* structure is important. *Of course* mathematics is important. Both, in fact, are essential in helping form the breakwater we need against the waves of change that crash upon our lives with increasing frequency. We will soon be making good use of each in establishing sound prescriptions for achieving balance.

But we should beware rigidity in our orbit, and also legalism in criticizing the orbit of another. The secret of balance is not found in enforced uniformity and legalistic rigidity. Instead it is achieved, first, in placing durable priorities at the center of our existence, and, second, placing our lives in a stable orbit around these same priorities.

Priorities:
From Trivial to Temporary to Timeless

If priorities are to be at the center of our personal solar system, we need to understand what this means. What kind of priorities have enough heft to keep us in orbit? What kind of wisely chosen core will transcend time and last all the way to our deathbed, and beyond?

People have placed a wide range of objects at the center of their orbits and attempted to build a life around them. In all, it constitutes quite a spectrum from the trivial to the temporary to the timeless.

Trivial Priorities
An old cartoon showed a politician at his desk, feet up, talking to his staff. "What do the polls say my core values are today?" Unfortunately, it isn't just politicians that fall into such ambiguity. Many of us have no idea what our priorities are. Perhaps even more tragic, many have settled for fluff.

Some, for instance, build their entire life around television. Snicker if you must, but it is more widespread than we care to admit. And with screens getting larger and the quality of transmission more and more life-like, the escape value of an electronic nest will only continue to grow. The entrancing effect of this type of media is undeniable. It is predicted that increasingly we will live in our own "virtual realities," consumed with visual effects, surround sound, and realistic olfactory and tactile sensations. If our work life is relentlessly stressful—which is already the case for millions—it will only be tolerated as a source of revenue and thus marginalized in our affections. Our real life will be the powerful and pleasurable fiction of the screen.

Others attempt to create a life around a pet, car, boat, house, motorcycle, sex, television, food, fashion, shopping, knitting, quilting, NASCAR, golfing, fishing, hunting, gardening, clothes, exercise, antiques, travel, social networking, the telephone, music, or sports. As a baseball fan for many decades, I can testify to the futility of attempting to balance one's life around the fortunes of the Chicago Cubs.

And what will our deathbed think of a life based on television, Twitter, or travel?

To be clear, there is nothing wrong with loving pets, music, gardens, or sports—I love them all. But we should not attempt to build a life around things that have no regal bearing, no transcendence, no soulful permanence. I have been in those rooms at the end and seen these people pass—believe me, you don't want to go there.

Temporary Priorities

There is another category of priority chosen by many, and it is well captured by the phrase "my priorities at the time." The implication is that when the circumstances of life change, priorities will also change. In essence, everything will be recalibrated. They will get a new sun and a new orbit in a new solar system.

To a certain extent, of course, we all change our focus as time passes depending on our circumstances. If we are in college, for example, our focus—our "priority at the time"—is to get good grades. If we have preschool children, our focus is to meet their needs. If we enter the workforce, our focus is to be an exceptional worker.

Unfortunately, we live in a world where everything changes continuously in a way never before experienced. To build a life on "my priorities at the time" is like building a house on the sand—the sand shifts, the house comes down. Yes, students should study hard, but in today's world, they often change colleges, or change majors, or drop out, or take a semester off, or graduate in a field they dislike—and it leaves them completely disoriented. Surely we should try to give our preschoolers a good start, but if we blink twice, they're on the way to kindergarten—what happens then? And the workforce? Jobs once thought stable are lost overnight, and the "job security office" now comes equipped with a revolving door.

Each of these temporary priorities is unarguably important. To do well in school, nurture our young children, and perform well at work—no one can dispute the importance of focusing on such efforts. Furthermore, these temporary priorities are vastly more worthy than those of the trivial variety.

Yet from a balance perspective, if the core priorities are not durable, they likely will contribute to the imbalance rather than solve it. Functionally speaking, it is more difficult to achieve balance when the context and surroundings are transient. The world is lurching enough as it is, and when we contribute to this problem by adding our own set of disruptions, we have compounded the problem. A center that shifts frequently cannot bear the onslaught of a culture where everything is disposable and expendable.

For example, a Bureau of Labor Statistics report stated that people hold an average of eleven jobs from age eighteen to forty-two.[3] Another study of employee tenure reports that "the median number of years that wage and salary workers had been with their current employer was 4.0 years."[4] When people change jobs, they also change employers, co-workers, commute circumstances, workplace routines, expectations, job descriptions, and sometimes even houses, neighbors, and communities. It is easy to see why balance has become so difficult today when change is epidemic on every front.

In the same way, balancing our lives will necessarily be difficult unless we have a stable orbit around a center with durability. It is little wonder people have trouble keeping their feet on the ground when they continuously switch out their center. They have not only a "balance problem" but also a "center problem."

Timeless Priorities

Contrast this with the stability of our solar system anchored by a sun whose mass is 333,000 times that of Earth. It is not a "temporary" sun,

1aranteed—it is not going anywhere. The integrity of our entire planetary relationship comes from this stable center—it gives us light, it sustains our life, it keeps us in orbit. When we wake up in the morning, it will be unchanged from when we went to bed.

Similarly, if our core priorities have a durability about them, we can build our life around this center without the need to repeatedly readjust.

For some, this is relationships. Upon their deathbed, they wish to be remembered as someone faithfully devoted to friends and family through-out all of life's circumstances. Notice the sense of transcendence here. This is not a priority based on preschool children, as precious as they are—because they only stay preschool for a few years. Rather it is the larger priority of being a person of love, service, and acceptance, whether to children, spouse, friends, neighbors, co-workers, and even strangers. This core does not need to be readjusted because of life's circumstances, for it is deeper and more compelling than any changing context and can penetrate directly into the next setting.

For others it is the realm of work and financial responsibility—a good work ethic regardless the job, debts quickly paid, generosity to those in need, and security for the family. Notice, once again, how this priority transcends change. The intention is to work hard, be honest and respect-ful in all dealings, charge only what is fair, have personal and professional integrity, be an example of frugality and thrift. These attributes are inter-nal, not external. No matter the circumstances, the opportunity exists to remain true to one's core priorities and to be guided by them.

For many, the center of their life is God. Of course, relationships and work are important here, but even more so because relationships and work are important to God. The love, service, acceptance, integrity, honesty, and respect mentioned above flow directly from the Scriptures. This center transcends all others, because even in the face of lost jobs, lost marriages, lost wealth, lost friendships, lost health, lost retirement, lost houses, and even lost children, God never changes, and He will never leave us or for-sake us.[5]

I, too, since 1969, have explicitly placed my life in stable orbit around the timeless center of God. In February of that year, while studying in

Basel, Switzerland, I traveled south for ten days to the French-speaking mountain town of Huémoz. At a small study center called L'Abri (*The Shelter*) run by Dr. Francis Schaeffer, I read, listened, discussed, studied, and prayed. On the outside, perhaps, my life looked fine—physics major with a premed emphasis, science awards, a beautiful and brilliant girlfriend back in the States (now long since my wife), spending a year studying humanities in beautiful alpine Switzerland. Yet the reality was different. Inside I was filled with an anguish that, at times, was excruciatingly painful, almost incapacitating.

I came to L'Abri, as did most, searching. At the end of ten days, as I prepared to leave, I made a unilateral decision. I decided to accept the Bible as the Word of God. A fellow student there (I don't recollect her name) was incensed. "You can't just do that!!" she almost screamed. "Well, maybe I can, and maybe I can't—but I'm going to just do that," I replied. Unfortunately, I never got to tell her the result. As I left Huémoz, within twenty-four hours, every shred of pain, anguish, doubt, or confusion disappeared. It was as if in a pitch-black home after an electrical storm, someone throws on the main circuit-breaker switch and floods the entire building with light, even spilling out through the windows and dazzling the yard. I once was blind, but now I saw. It was overwhelming, really.

It has been forty years, yet the reality is fresh and unchanged. It is little wonder, then, that God, truth, and love are the durable priorities at the center of my orbit. Everything flows from this eternal timeless center, everything relates to this center, everything connects to this center. God, truth, and love do not change, and therefore I never need to shift or redefine. Balance is much easier under such conditions.

Over time, my orbit has taken many different directions. Right now, for example, I am writing this book, and while it's been a fourteen-month effort, at present the entire summer is given over to this project. In September, my speaking schedule picks up again and is quite full. Later, I will do more dedicated research on trends. Is this balanced living? Yes, it is. For even if I speed up or slow down, even if I am speaking or writing or researching, even if I am at home or on the road, my priorities remain precisely the same. In private practice, in academic medicine, or as a watchman on the wall—each career, each transition, each activity relates to the center in exactly the same way.

If I write a book, it is not simply because it seems like a good idea at the time. I only write books when the timing and topic are thoroughly consistent with God, truth, and love. When I speak, travel, research, practice medicine, or teach residents, it is only because I have spiritual peace and clearness in pursuing the activity. The pace, balance, and load of my work are determined in the same way. I limit my schedule. I don't allow pressure to force my hand. When needed, I say no quickly and easily. God is a God of order, peace, depth, and contentment, not irritability, frustration, disorganization, and burnout.

In all of this, I am carefully preparing for my deathbed. Rather than a mournful duty, it actually is quite enjoyable. It is not a burden but a freedom. It is a profound existential relief to know that my orbit is correct, that the center is well chosen, and that at the end of this path is a bed without terminal regret.

Author Kathleen Norris has written, "I know for sure that at the end, the playful stranger who appears is not death but love." The day will come when I will say goodbye, slide through that veil, and be greeted by Love. I have no fear.

Nico's Final Day

For older people to disappear through the veil is one thing; for a child, it is something completely different. Nothing in all of medicine is more difficult than the death of a child. And nothing in all of medicine or life is more difficult than the death of your own child. June 3, 2008, we lost our beloved eleven-month-old grandson to rare surgical complications. He was not supposed to die.

Nico Everett Swenson was born 7-7-07 on the seventh day of the week. These are holy numbers, and from the beginning he seemed protected. He survived drama and death repeatedly until it seemed a pattern: cervical incompetence at twenty-weeks gestation, dangerous funneling of the amniotic membranes, rescue cerclage with 15 percent chance of success, multiple episodes of premature labor, possible amnionitis, possible rupture of membranes, repeated medication reactions, premature delivery at thirty-three weeks, respirator in the Neonatal ICU.

But then he came home with Adam, Maureen, and sister, Katja, healthy and happy and became simply "our sweet Nico." He was everything a perfect baby should be, and we rejoiced together.

It wasn't until two months that a heart murmur was heard. The investigation revealed an atrial septal defect with leakage in two valves. Surgery was planned for one year of age—a time far off and unforeboding. He grew, smiled, cooed, played, and all the while delighted in his sister's fondness for him.

Thursday, April 24: The surgical day came without much anxiety—it should be five days and out. But something went horribly wrong. He hemorrhaged through his ventricular wall in a way the cardiologist had never seen before. They almost lost him. Not surprisingly, he cheated death once again and made it back to the unit. Hooked up to a external heart pump (ECMO) and respirator, he was medicated for sedation, eyes closed. His beautiful eyelashes were striking.

Monday, April 28: His condition worsened. The mitral valve leakage was severe and untenable. The nurses cried. They ran him back to OR. The surgeon returned with a smile. "Things went well."

Saturday, May 3: "It's still an article of faith," wrote Adam, "that this little guy on the bed is our Nico. He's just so inert, his chest rising and falling with the mechanical puff of the ventilator, his eyes hooded and sleepy. He should be grabbing at everything in sight and chewing on Maureen's hair. We have to have faith, that when he finally awakes, he will."

The valves began leaking more, his cardiac function deteriorated, his kidneys backed up. Prayer meetings bedside, prayer meetings in the church, prayer meetings around the world, in Paraguay, Kurdistan, and Afghanistan where aid workers prayed "against the insurgency and that Nico would pee like a racehorse." The choices were now grim—heart transplant or mechanical valve.

Monday, May 19: Despite horrible risk statistics regarding clots—50 percent mortality the first year—the mechanical valve was chosen as his only realistic option. The valve seated nicely, and the procedure gave a renewed sense of hope.

For sixteen days and 2,304,000 clicks, the mitral valve opened and closed as designed. Slowly the medical staff began weaning him from the respirator and narcotics. His tube feedings increased, his kidney function improved, he had more movement.

Tuesday, June 3: In the sudden early-morning hours, Nico's earthly journey came to an end. A massive clot plugged the mitral valve. Adam wrote: "We counted that we had almost lost Nico fourteen times before this . . . This time was the fifteenth time, and as I sat in the waiting room at 6:15 this morning, I was utterly numb. I walked in to say goodbye to him while they were doing compressions. He was blue. I kissed his head over and over and tried to tell him we loved him while they pushed on his chest again and again to keep him alive. I'm not sure if he heard me or not. I like to think he did."

They let us stay with his body for six hours before taking him away. We kissed him so many times, our beautiful, broken departed baby.

As Nico climbed into his tiny boat and crossed the Jordan, we stared into the mists rising from the river. Our brains stopped thinking, the clocks stopped ticking, the world stopped spinning, the earth stood still. We all understood instantly and together—from his deathbed, our little buddy had given us the gift of knowing *exactly* what matters most.

Now it was up to us to live it.

(This eulogy, written by Adam, was read by their pastor at Nico's funeral.)

Nico Everett Swenson
7.7.07–6.3.08
A Lament

I am a father without a son.

This is a desperately wrong state of affairs. We, all of us, live in a world that is suddenly without Nico Everett Swenson. This world is immeasurably worse than the one that existed on Monday, June 2nd. I'm sorry for that, I apologize from the depths of my heart, but we did everything we could, everyone did. The greatest medical care in the world notwithstanding, some of them just don't make it.

I hear that Nico is in a better place now, a perfect place free of tubes and monitors and wires. I hear myself saying that Nico is with Jesus now, and I believe this in the abstract, though it is so very hard to understand.

Right now I'm too wrecked to understand much of anything. Right now a simple photograph will bring me to my knees. Right now the glimpse of his crib through an open door just destroys me. Right now I wish to control so many things that I can't. My son has completed his earthly journey—ashes to ashes, dust to dust. I don't understand a world without Nico.

All of this saddens me more than I can tell you.

But let's get one thing straight. I'm sad for you, I'm sad for me, I'm sad for Maureen, for Katja. Nico's spirit has departed. Nico is happy now. He is healthy. This is what I believe and seek to understand.

Many of you never got to meet Nico. We had to quarantine him, to protect him from illness. He was a preemie after all, a preemie with a heart condition. Many of you never got to see his twinkling eyes or his two tooth smile. Many of you never got to hear his hearty laugh, or witness his repertoire of party tricks, which relied heavily on giggling and toe-chomping. I'm sorry for that too. He really was a great kid. He was beautiful, compassionate, and perceptive. He was a fighter.

I wanted so much to see what he'd be like as a four-year-old, as an eight-year-old, as an eighteen-year-old. If Katja is any indication, I think he'd have been amazing. I wanted to read the books he'd write, and listen to him play the guitar out on the back deck. I wanted to talk with him, man to man, in the fishing boat. I wanted to be a slow, old first baseman while he darted around left field robbing home runs and throwing out baserunners. I know you all wanted that too. I'm sorry it won't happen. We tried, really we did.

I can't tell you why he died. I wish I could. Well, I can tell you one reason: a massive blood clot blocked up his mechanical valve. His medical team was vigilant, they did compressions until all hope was lost. We tried to thank them the best we could, given the circumstances. We tried to let them off the hook.

I know that reason. The one I don't understand, and probably never will, is the larger question, the metaphysical quandary. Why does a father outlive his son? Whose idea was that? Why does a world so in need of grace and truth and beauty lose someone who clearly loved so much? And what are the rest of us supposed to do now?

I know I'm asking questions way beyond my pay grade, but I can't help it.

Socrates said that anyone seeking pleasure would find pain comingled with it. C. S. Lewis said that pain is "God's megaphone to rouse a deaf world." Well, he certainly has my attention. We're talking now: it's an alternatingly weepy and angry conversation (and probably not too coherent on my end), but we're talking. I still trust him. I still trust that he is good. I still trust that, somehow, he has our best in all of this. I trust that he loves me as a father loves a son, that his heart breaks as mine does.

I understand that Nico was a gift to us, one that we were able to cherish for four days shy of eleven months. I understand now that there are no guarantees, and that we had better love with abandon for what's around the corner is not ours to know.

I understand that when we make babies, we don't really have a say in what we get. If we'd been able to check off an order form for Nico, to go down line by line and fill it out, I'm pretty sure we'd have passed on the bum ticker. But the genetic combination that resulted in our beautiful, inquisitive, sweet-tempered, blue-eyed boy also featured a partial Atrial Ventricular Septal Defect in a heart whose upper-left chamber was two standard deviations too small. That's the deal. Take it or leave it.

Anyone in the same room with Nico for one minute understood that he was a perfect baby. People told us all the time that he was strikingly handsome, that his smile was so darling, that his eyes were so blue, that his hair was so thick. He was all the things a baby was supposed to be. He was our sweet boy, bum ticker and all.

I don't understand why Nico had to come with the heart he did. I don't understand why he was taken from us now, when we still had so much love to give. But I do understand that, unbearable as the pain is now, the pleasure, the love, and the joy he brought into my life was infinitely more. I understand that as acute as the suffering is, and as bleak as the world is now, it was worth it to know him for 10 months and 27 days.

We miss you, sweet boy. Can't wait to see you again.

All my love,
Dad

HOW TO COUPLE BALANCE (*EQUILIBRIUM*) WITH MARGIN (*CAPACITY*)

TWENTY-TWO-YEAR-old R&B singer and actress Aaliyah should not have trusted her entourage. But when you're an emerging superstar with number-one recordings, album sales totaling twenty-four million, Grammy nominations, and major film contracts, it's the big time and you have places to go and things to do. So it's off to the Bahamas for a video shoot, over to Miami, then up to New York.

They finished the filming early and decided to return to the mainland that same evening. Loading the plane at Marsh Harbour, the baggage handlers complained that the luggage—including cameras and sound equipment—exceeded weight restrictions. The pilot, too, protested that it was too much weight for a safe flight. But this being his first day on the job, pilot Morales undoubtedly did not wish to attract attention, considering his falsified records, lack of certification for a Cessna 420B, and the traces of cocaine and alcohol in his blood. Aaliyah's Los Angeles-based staff insisted that they paid for the charter and everything must be loaded.

The twin-engine, single-pilot Cessna was rated for eight passengers. They had nine. The plane, fuel, and baggage totaled 5,500 pounds, leaving 800 pounds for the passengers. Once the 300-pound bodyguard climbed on board, that left 62 pounds apiece for the remaining six men and two women.

The plane climbed a mere fifty feet into the air, then crashed nose first. All nine died. Aaliyah's career ended 200 feet beyond the runway in a boggy marsh. At least one bag descended into the ooze and was never recovered.

According to the National Transportation Safety Board (NTSB), "The total gross weight of the plane was substantially exceeded. Preliminary center of gravity calculations showed that the center of gravity was significantly outside the flight envelope past the aft center of gravity."[1] In other words, the problem was not only the extra weight but also the imbalance —the center of gravity was pushed too far back toward the tail.

The formula is straightforward: Overload + Imbalance + Flying = Death.

Imbalance, Overload, and the Rapidly Approaching Ground

Balance has to do with equilibrium; margin has to do with load. Both are well-respected issues in the aviation industry. They are studied, taught, required, regulated, feared, and even preached.

And, sometimes, they are ignored.

Analyzing the Aaliyah calamity, John Frank, executive director of the Cessna Pilots' Association, said, "Every nook and cranny of that airplane was packed." The *placement* of the cargo, he explained, was as important as the weight, because a tail-heavy load can cause a pilot to lose control. "When you start talking about control, weight doesn't matter so much, although it makes it harder to fly. Control is based on where the weight is placed."[2]

In 1982, popular and highly respected Christian singer-songwriter Keith Green offered to take friends on a sightseeing flight over his ministry properties in east Texas. Twelve people—four adults and eight children—climbed into a leased Cessna 414 that had only seven seats. The pilot, Don Burmaster, a former Marine aviator, taxied down the private airstrip and lifted off. But the plane oscillated violently and crashed into thirty-foot high trees less than a mile away. The NTSB determined the tragedy was due to a 450-pound overload with the center of gravity four and a half inches rear of the maximum aft limits. Perhaps a contributing factor was that in the Marines, weight and balance responsibilities fall to the loadmaster and not the pilot, thus Burmaster might have neglected this aspect of flying by habit.[3] Among the dead were twenty-eight-year-old Green, his three-year-old son Josiah, and his two-year-old daughter Bethany.

In 2005, a luxury charter plane belonging to Platinum Jet Management attempted takeoff from the Teterboro, New Jersey, airport near New York City. Instead, it crashed through a fence, skidded across Route 46 during rush hour, hit several cars shearing the roof off one, and slammed into a clothing warehouse. The high-end service, charging as much as $90,000 per flight, routinely catered to celebrities such as Bill Clinton, George H. W. Bush, Shaquille O'Neal, Joe Montana, and Beyoncé. Upon investigation, the now defunct—and indicted—company admitted to secretly loading up jet fuel by topping off tanks at airports where it was cheaper. Then they would routinely lie about centers of gravity, which were too far forward because of this "tankering scheme." The Teterboro flight that crashed had a dangerous weight configuration at takeoff, and fuel overload was the primary contributing factor in the accident.

In 2009, a devastating crash near Butte, Montana, ended the lives of fourteen close California friends on their way to a skiing vacation at a Big Sky resort. The six parents, seven children, and one pilot were aboard a Pilatus PC-12 designed for a maximum of ten. Weather might also have been a contributing factor.

On New Year's Eve, 1972, a chartered DC-6 carrying baseball Hall of Famer Roberto Clemente crashed a few minutes after taking off from Luis Muñoz Marin International Airport in San Juan, Puerto Rico. Clemente, an esteemed athlete and humanitarian, was flying as part of a relief effort for Nicaraguan earthquake victims. Neither the bodies nor the plane's wreckage were ever found. An overload of supplies was blamed for the airplane's accident.

An attorney discussing flying said that some pilots treat their planes as pickup trucks, piling things in and loading them up without a second thought. "If you think the plane might be overloaded, it never hurts to ask the pilot for the numbers. If the pilot says, '. . . P'shaw, a bit of overloading is never a problem, these planes are built to take it . . .' don't set foot in the plane."[4]

Sometimes, though, we treat our lives like that pickup truck rather than an airplane. We stack it high, fill every nook and cranny, cram it to the gills. Then, perhaps, we survive the situation with no problem. When confidence leads to overconfidence, we load even more, we pack it even higher, and we speed even faster. Once again, we arrive intact—and that policeman only gave us a warning.

Inside our abdomen, however, somewhere down in our duodenum, we have a niggling feeling that maybe we miscalculated. How do we otherwise explain these rising stress levels, increasing symptoms, and compounding consequences? Almost before we know it, we find ourselves knee-deep in accelerating risk—looming deadlines, monstrous mortgages, sleepless nights, soaring debt, strained relationships. Our pickup, it turns out, was in fact a single-engine plane that we only *treated* like a truck. Now we're at ten thousand feet, looking around the cockpit for some margin and balance because at these heights, error is unforgiving. There's no redundancy, no fail-safe, no parachutes, no government bailouts—only the rapidly approaching earth below.

Margin as a Spectrum; Balance as a Beam

These crash scenarios demonstrate how overload and imbalance are often related. For example, if the plane is too full (overloaded, with no margin) and the center of gravity is too far back (out of balance), it will likely stall at takeoff. This is worse than it sounds and not the best way to impress your passengers.

But when the principles of margin and balance are appropriately applied, we are rewarded with the exhilaration of soaring into the heavens, floating among the clouds, and surveying the diminishing earth below. It is one of the truly magnificent advantages of modern progress.

In the larger context, beyond the application in aviation, *margin is about making space* for the things that matter most, while *balance is about preserving space* for the things that matter most. The two concepts are independent, yet they fit together so well we might fairly consider them siblings. Their applicability extends to nearly every aspect of life, both on the positive side (margin and balance are therapeutic and freedom-giving) and the negative side (overload and imbalance are painful and burdensome).

The Margin Spectrum

Margin is a concept about capacity and load, and can be represented by a spectrum.

- If we are at *80 percent capacity*, we have margin in our lives. There is some space between our load and our limits, some gas in the tank, some money in the bank.
- If we are at *100 percent capacity*, we are maximized. We are topped out, and we have no wiggle room, no reserves, no buffer, no leeway. There is no margin left for error.
- If we are at *120 percent capacity*, we are overloaded. We have moved beyond the threshold now and are well into a negative capacity setting.

These three numbers are, of course, somewhat arbitrary. We could also have chosen 90-100-110 or perhaps 50-100-150. But whatever the numbers, they help illustrate the spectrum implicit within the margin concept. It is a continuum from excess capacity, to no capacity, to negative capacity.

When margined, we have *excess* capacity—we have space in our pickup or our plane for more passengers and luggage. No problem, glad to have you. Don't worry. We won't crash. We always obey the weight restrictions.

When maximized, we have *no additional* capacity. The plane is full and we'll be fine, but we're not taking that suitcase over there because it can't fit safely—you will have to ship it—no, sorry, you might be a 300-pound bodyguard, but we just can't do it; or the hotel is full, and the "no vacancy" sign is out—there are no more beds, sorry; or the bank statement just arrived and we have enough to pay our bills, but that's it—no McDonald's this month—so let's hope nothing breaks down and nobody chips a tooth.

When overloaded, we have *negative* capacity. All our space is gone, our reserves are used up, our accounts are depleted, our capacity is consumed, and we're running on fumes. Actually, for some, it's kind of exciting to be out on a limb—a challenge, an adrenaline latte, a chance to grow, to prove oneself, to differentiate oneself from the crowd. No pain, no gain, right? We're good at speed, and we're great at multitasking. We'll just take a few shortcuts and delist a few of our friends. Sleep? We can do that when we're dead.

There are many different responses to overload, from those who decompensate into a collapsing puddle of worry, to those who charge directly into the teeth of the storm with a grin on their faces. But it is important that we hold to the definitions. By definition, if we are overloaded, we are overloaded, and that means dysfunction. If we remain in this condition for a period of time, reliably, things will go wrong. Some may say, "I do fine at 120 percent," but if that is the case, they are cheating on the definitions. If they are thriving at 120 percent, then they must downgrade the 120 percent to 100 percent or 90 percent (or else start being more perceptive about their dysfunctional symptoms). We can't call it true overload unless there is an associated dysfunction over time.

The Balance Beam

Balance is a concept about equilibrium, and one representation might be a balance beam. If we successfully stay on the beam, we are in balance. If we fall off, we are out of balance. Notice that this is quite different than the margin spectrum.

A standard balance beam is four inches wide, four feet off the ground, and sixteen feet long. But, if we wish, we can make the beam as narrow as a wire or as wide as a driveway. We can remove the supports and put it on the floor. We can even make it a plank twelve inches wide. The point is, we are either on it or we are off it. We are either successfully balanced or we are out of balance.

To be on a balance beam does not mean we get to wander all around the countryside. We must be on the beam, however wide we define it. We must maintain our equilibrium and keep an even keel.

In the previous chapter, we defined balance as a stable, reliable orbit around our core priorities. This implies steadiness, constancy, imperturbability, and it even implies purpose, because our balanced orbit always relates to the core priorities. We dispensed with unnecessary rigidity and legalism—and rightly so—but that does not mean we can abandon all standards. If we wish a balanced life, we may not break orbit and go dancing around another galaxy for a decade. That's not balance; it's anarchy.

Perhaps it is now time to take our balance beam and stretch it into that orbit around our priorities. We will make it comfortably wide so we can have some latitude, sufficiently smooth so we can speed up or slow down, and even bi-directional so we can travel to the right or left. But if we wish balance, we will stay in our orbit. And, most importantly, we will shape our orbit in a way that it always remains in view of the center, for it is this center that contains the things that matter most.

The Margin-Balance Partnership

Once we choose a margin setting for our lives—a level we think might keep us productive at work but also allow for the deeper and mellower aspects of life—we will discover a hard truth. It is very difficult to keep margin within a narrow range. Perhaps we think that 80 percent sounds wonderful, but then we slide all over the place, from 80 to 98 to 92 to 128 to 105. I have already said repeatedly that our era is volatile and unstable, and there are well-researched reasons why this is so. But the consequence is that it becomes difficult for us to hold our course. The weather is stormy, the seas are high, and we find ourselves thrown around the ocean like a cork.

This is where balance comes in. If we want to live a margined life perhaps in a range of 75 to 90 percent or 80 to 95 percent, balance will help us secure our equilibrium around these levels. It provides a keel to keep us straight, a rudder to keep us on course, and ballast to guarantee our center of gravity.

While margin *creates* a space in our lives for the things that matter most, balance *preserves* that space in our lives for the things that matter most. Our core priorities *are themselves* the things that matter most, and they recline, even now, on our deathbed awaiting our arrival.

Margin, Profusion, and the Load Limit of Life

I have written four books on the topic of margin and have concluded it is time to give margin some assistance in its battle against overload. Balance offers its own unique contribution to the cause. Margin helps us develop some reserves; balance helps us stabilize our reserves. The margin concept helps us choose what level of capacity works best for us; the balance concept helps us maintain equilibrium and steadiness at our chosen capacity level. Margin helps us keep our balance; balance helps us preserve our margin.

Together, margin and balance build a stronger edifice against the overload juggernaut. In the future we will wish to employ both of these tools in tandem. But since the remainder of this book is dedicated to providing scores of practical prescriptions for enhancing our balance, perhaps it will be helpful here to take a few pages and explain margin in more detail.

It has already been emphasized repeatedly that we ought not underestimate the remarkable conditions facing us today. We live in a pregnant age. Unprecedented change hangs heavy in the air, marked by the kind of mathematics never before seen. The future looms large, imposing, full of certain blessings yet undeniable threats. Optimists rejoice at the expectant bounty, while pessimists cower at imminent collapse.

Some features of this future are to be welcomed, others resisted: the rapid dissemination of technology, the promising yet frightening biomedical ethical developments, the entrancing dominance of media, the rapidly shifting traditions and social mores, the increasingly dysfunctional worldwide demographic patterns, the vulnerabilities and complexities of a globally integrated economic system, our overwhelming future entitlement debt, the democratization of power for purposes of both good and evil, and the exponential profusion on all fronts. This is only a partial list, but it's still enough to cross a rabbi's eyes.

Such conditions are sufficient to swat about even the strongest among us, and this is why balance and margin have been enlisted to help us guard not only our priorities and relationships but also our joy, our freedom, and our sanity. In that regard, it is the last item in the above paragraph—the exponential profusion—that we need to revisit.

If you will remember, profusion is the name given to the phenomenon of "more." Over the past thirty years, we have seen this curve turn vertical, and the graph of Profusion over Time (see page 38) is unique in all of historical experience. Never before has it been conceptually plotted, and never before have the implications been considered.

Many have grown casual, even resistant, to dramatic statements, vertical graphs, and endless assertions of danger. The reader is, of course, free to develop his or her own opinion on the matter, but neglect of the issue does not constitute a functional exemption from the consequences of what will happen at the hands of this significant force. So whether we understand it or not, whether we respect it or not, profusion will dominate our future in unavoidable ways.

It is fully appropriate to celebrate the positive implications of profusion, and there are many to celebrate. But I am mostly concerned about the negative implications. Here we will only consider those negatives that pertain to the collision between profusion and limits, specifically because of how that collision is so harmful to the margin we need.

Every human has limits. For example, each of us has limits in physical strength, emotional resilience, intellectual capacity, performance productivity, time, and finances. These limits are relatively fixed.

For millennia, these fixed limits have not been an issue because civilization simply defined itself around this reality. We could not work much after dark because there was little artificial light; we slept nine and a half hours per night because the only alternative was starring at a pitch-black wall; we could seldom go into debt because there was no one to lend us money, there were few things to buy, and plastic had not yet been invented; we never breached our intellectual limits because there were few schools and few books, and most people were illiterate.

Around 1750, this began to change. And, most notably, over the last thirty years the world turned upside down.

During these past few decades, profusion doubled, then doubled again. Then it doubled again and again and again. Of course this was exciting, and we stood on the sidelines, eyes glistening, watching the glorious parade of unending products and rising prosperity.

The problem was our intellectual capacity and emotional resilience could not multiply to keep up. Our physical energy was strained by shortened sleep, longer commutes, and heavier work demands. Our finances took a hit because in every mailbox was a new credit card offering to loan us the money we need to buy stuff we didn't need. And the twenty-four-hour day stubbornly refused to expand. In short, the profusion of progress led to steadily increasing pressure on our margins.

One might guess that, sensing our plight, profusion would take pity. Perhaps when progress saw that our margin was disappearing like oxygen in a scuttled submarine, it might slow down and give us a chance to adjust. Nice theory, but it will never happen. Progress has its own agenda and will never stop to worry about our limits. Its sole job is to give us more and more of everything faster and faster. To slow or to stop would destroy our economy, and to date, this lacks bipartisan support.

So the profusion of progress will continue to increase, and our margin in emotional energy, physical energy, time, and finances will continue to decrease. Most of us now live beyond the threshold of our limits in one or several areas, and we routinely spend more than we have whether in money, time, or energy. Maximizing everything has become the American way—we push the limits as far as possible, then we push some more. When life is continuously maximized, however, there is no margin for priorities, relationship, healing, depth, rest, service, contemplation, or worship. Essentially, for all the things that matter most.

As a result, life in modern-day America is essentially devoid of time and space. Not the *Star Trek* kind—the sanity kind. Overload is the new normal. We have too many choices and decisions, too many activities and commitments, too much change creating too much stress. We have too much speed and hurry. We have too much technology, complexity, traffic, information, possessions, debt, expectations, advertisements, and media. And we have too little margin.

But if overload is the disease, then margin is the antidote. To balance today's lifestyles, restoring our margin is a needed first step. The vast majority of us are healthier if we draw a line somewhere short of overload, i.e., if we preserve some margin. Therapeutically, restoring margin to one's life often relieves the pain. Life comes alive again.

Margin is a simple principle. For example, we do not follow two inches behind the car in front of us or allow only two minutes to change planes in Chicago—that would leave no margin for error. We don't begrudge the margin on a page. Why then do we insist on leaving no space, no reserves in our day to day?

There was a time when people had margin in their lives. People lingered at the dinner table, helped the kids with homework, visited with the neighbors, took long walks, dug in the garden, slept full nights, and took weekends off. None of this was regarded as unusual.

Those were the days when progress was mellow. Today, however, progress is different—it's aggressive and turbocharged. This is the genesis of our margin problem. As long as the *more* of progress does not threaten our limits, we are thrilled with its bounty. But once the *more* of progress collides with the established fact of human limits—which it inevitably does—the situation changes. At that point, we become stressed and overstimulated. The demands upon us exceed our reserves, and our margin slips away.

When our margin is depleted and our reserves are gone, we shift emphasis. Instead of being compassionate and caring in our attitude, we become apathetic or rude. Instead of being outwardly focused in our service, we become self-protective. Instead of pursuing innovation and productivity in our job, we become irritable and fatigued.

Let's look at how this works with our performance limits, for example.

The Human Function Curve[5] shows the relationship between *stress* (x-axis) and *productivity* (y-axis). When stress levels are low—little change, challenge, novelty, responsibility, demand, or deadlines—our productivity is also low. But as the stress levels increase, our productivity climbs rapidly. Then, at Point A—that infamous point of diminishing returns—our productivity flattens. If stress continues beyond this point, productivity declines. Notice the appearance of fatigue in the vertically shaded area, followed by exhaustion in the horizontally shaded area, and then burnout.

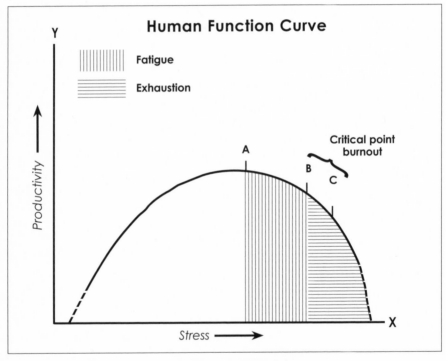

Stress Versus Productivity

The implications of this graph are enormous. It is a wonderful privilege to have productive activity. But, on the other hand, to push beyond our limits is not only unsustainable but will also lead to decreasing levels of productivity. Margin is productivity with sustainability, while overload is productivity with exhaustion and burnout.

Nationally known consultant and author Marty Nemko advises:

Don't give 110 percent. I have a client who always gives 110 percent. Yes, he reaps rewards, but he's stressed out much of the time, makes mistakes as a result, and hasn't developed close relationships. The most successful people I know give 90 percent. They stay in the moment, tackle their projects slowly but steadily, and don't waste time worrying about what's ahead. They also have the emotional reserves to develop relationships and enjoy work.[6]

Without margin, instead of completing tasks, we're buried in disorganization and frustration. Without margin, energy is replaced by exhaustion. Without margin, instead of fixing problems, we become the problem. Without margin, instead of helping people, we avoid them. Without margin, hearing of yet "one more opportunity to serve" sounds like a penalty rather than a blessing. It is hard to carry one another's burdens when we can't even make it through the day ourselves.

What happens when overload collides with the family? Many well-intentioned homes are exhausted and overwhelmed, driven by powerful cultural forces. Families live on a treadmill, are besieged by routine panic, and are run over by high-speed good intentions. Stress levels in parents often flow downhill, engulfing the kids. Healthy families, on the other hand, create a margin to facilitate relational well-being. Margin restores what culture has taken away: time to listen, strength to care, space to love.

What happens when overload collides with faith? We become too busy to pray or serve and too exhausted for relationships. Irritability poisons our attitude, and burnout lurks around every corner. God gets the busy signal. Joy is an early casualty. Even the church is now officially "too busy for God."[7]

Margin sends us down the path in the opposite direction. Margin advises us to create some buffers and guard our borders. As we carve out margin in emotional energy, physical energy, time, and finances, our resilience is strengthened. Buoyancy returns. Reserves are built up. Relationships are energized. Our batteries are recharged. And we actually become *more* available for the purposes of God.

Margin, rightly conceived, is not about laziness, mediocrity, and noninvolvement. It is about focus, discipline, and self-control. But mostly it is a prioritizing space where we concentrate on the things that matter most.

Restoring margin to overloaded lives is possible if we are willing to think creatively, live differently, act intentionally, and stop following the crowds to the malls. Hundreds of practical margin suggestions have been written elsewhere to assist in such a lifestyle direction. But the first step, as always, resides within each human heart.

$$/ / / /$$

Did you know that if Mt. Everest had a staircase, it would contain 49,762 steps? That's like walking up the Empire State Building twenty-three times. Swimming the English Channel takes 50,000 strokes and over twelve hours, and it's regarded as more difficult than Everest.

Confronting the imbalance and overload of our age is a different kind of endurance struggle, and one that is often underestimated. The same forces of modernity that have combined to produce our "all-stress-all-the-time, switching-focus-at-lightning-speed, constant-rebalancing" age are virtually guaranteed to continue their rising trajectory.

An understanding of balance, margin, boundaries, and stress management will help. A firm dedication to long-term priorities is absolutely essential. And God is ready to do His part as well, for He long ago endorsed the kind of green pastures and still waters where He restoreth our soul.[8]

The next section of the book will present practical prescriptions to be employed as appropriate to the unique context of each life. These prescriptions are like little birds.

The story is told of an old hermit who lived high on a mountain. The reports of his wisdom circulated far and wide, bringing many to the door of his cabin. It was a long and difficult trek, and the old man spoke but few words. Yet in each instance, the people came away marveling at the wisdom they'd received.

Three troubled boys in the village saw the hermit during his monthly trip below and were annoyed at this reputation. He is just a stupid old man, they said. Together they decided to make the climb and present the hermit with an impossible problem. But each time, they came away frustrated. Finally, the oldest boy discovered a foolproof plan. "I'll catch a bird and we'll bring it to the hermit behind my back. When he comes to the door, we'll ask him what I have in my hands. If he guesses a bird, I will ask, 'What kind of bird?' If he guesses a sparrow, I will ask, 'Is it alive or dead?' If he says dead, I will release the bird and prove him wrong. If he says alive, I'll crush the sparrow and show him the dead bird."

Gleefully they set out. Along the way, they captured a tiny sparrow and put it in a cage. As they neared the cabin, the older boy removed the bird from the cage and put it behind his back. They knocked on the door, then heard the old man's stick hitting the floor as he shuffled. The door opened, and the hermit studied each face, slowly, one at a time. The oldest boy shifted his weight, then said, "Old man, what do I have behind my back?" "A bird," the hermit replied. "That is correct—what kind of bird?" the boy asked. "A tiny sparrow," the hermit replied. "Once again, that is correct. And is the sparrow alive or dead?" the boy asked with a wicked grin.

The old man looked directly into his eyes and said, "It is as you will."

PART TWO

COUNTERING THE ESCALATION OF THE NORM

ONE OF OUR sons recently bought a used car from a nice young man in South Dakota. It was a simple transaction and not a lot of money was exchanged. They shook hands, waved goodbye, and that was it. It didn't take long—but it was long enough to find out why he was selling the car. This thirty-two-year-old's life had fallen off a cliff. He had a job with real estate in a prosperous area of the Midwest that earned him $200,000 to $400,000 a year. What do you do with that kind of money? You buy some cars and trucks, and you get yourself a $1.2 million home. If nothing else, it's at least in keeping with the spirit of our age. But when the housing market collapsed, everything went south overnight. He lost his job, his house, and now was selling his last car (he did keep his truck). His wife had just given birth to their third child a few days ago—all under three years of age—so they moved in with in-laws to regroup.

Compare that to another midwesterner. Born in Omaha in 1930, Warren Buffett is on-again, off-again the world's richest man and arguably the greatest investor in American history. In 1958, at the age of twenty-seven, he bought a gray stucco house in Omaha for $31,500 and lives in it to this day. The house has appreciated through the years and is now valued at $700,000, but in comparison, that's still only half the cost of the home recently lost by our young ex-realtor.

The Oracle of Omaha is notoriously frugal. He eats at Dairy Queen, loves burgers and Cherry Coke (fifteen cans a day, bought by the case), plays the ukulele, and drives himself one-and-a-half miles daily to his modest office. He sits down at the same desk that belonged to his father at precisely 8:30 a.m. and goes home at 5:30 p.m. He shuns high society and instead makes popcorn at home, watches some television, and plays bridge on his computer. His advice is to live your life as simple as you are, just wear those things in which you feel comfortable, and don't waste money on unnecessary items.

What does a multibillionaire and one of *Time Magazine*'s 100 Most Influential People in the World (2007) say about success? "Basically, when you get to my age, you'll measure your success in life by how many of the people you want to love you actually do love you. If you get to my age in life and nobody thinks well of you, I don't care how big your bank balance is, your life is a disaster."[1] In another setting, he gave the same message in slightly different terms: "If people get to my age and they have the people love them that they want to have love them, they're successful. *It doesn't make any difference if they've got a thousand dollars in the bank or a billion dollars in the bank* [emphasis added]."[2]

To keep this bipartisan (Buffett being a staunch Democrat), let's head west to find a conservative example of a famous man in a simple house. In 1974, shortly before completing his second term as governor of California, Ronald and Nancy Reagan bought the Rancho del Cielo thirty miles north of Santa Barbara. Nestled in the mountains in a remote location with difficult access roads, this *Ranch of the Sky* served as the Reagan home from 1974 until 1995. It was even used for vacations during his two presidential terms, thus earning its nickname the Western White House. The most powerful man in the world felt most at home in a 1,500-square-foot modest adobe ranch house that was a hundred years old.

Reagan would exchange his coat and tie for jeans and a workshirt and then spend the day cutting brush, fixing fences, laying patio stones, reroofing the home with red Spanish tiles, and wading into the pond to catch water snakes. Here he hosted a disapproving Mikhail Gorbachev—"*Nekulturny*" the Russians would say, not cultured activities for a leader. He also received

Margaret Thatcher and even entertained Queen Elizabeth during a pouring rainstorm. The house was decorated with simple furnishings: rattan armchairs, a plain wooden dining-room table, Indian rugs on whitewashed walls, an oak loveseat rocker, a den with a tile floor and sheepskin rugs.[3]

We have quite a contrast in these three examples. Why would a young man, after only a few years in the workforce, rush to a luxury lifestyle with all its big-ticket trappings—the kind of life and level of possessions his parents could not have achieved even after fifty years of working? Where did he develop such a generational leap-frogging expectation, disregarding the ancestral tradition of beginning with a starter home? When both "the greatest investor in the history of America" and "the most powerful man in the world" were content with simplicity, why did our young friend lavish himself with top-of-the-line digs?

We live in the age of the escalating norm. For whatever reason, people want bigger, better, and fancier without regard to cost, consequences, or contentment. Of course we've always had a tendency to grab upward—but never at the levels seen today.

And its effect on balance has been devastating.

Escalation and Normalization

What we are witnessing is a continuous *escalation of the norm* followed rapidly by a *normalization of the escalation* that then becomes *the new normal*. At some point, if we wish to get our balance back—to say nothing of our economic stability or even our common sense—we will need to confront this pattern.

Hebert Stein, chairman of the Council of Economic Advisers under Nixon and Ford, developed Herbert Stein's Law: "If something cannot go on forever, it will stop."[4] The Government Accountability Office came up with a corollary law in a 2007 report warning of the dangers of long-term fiscal irresponsibility: "By definition, what is unsustainable will not be sustained."[5]

The application of these laws to our continuously upward trajectory of normal implies that "the escalation of the norm cannot be sustained, it cannot go on forever, and it will not go on forever." The only question is whether it will be stopped by wisdom or by crisis.

A driving force in this relentless escalation of the norm is our steadily rising expectations. Since progress has been so obliging in giving us more and more of everything faster and faster, we have come to expect more. And of course, our advertising industry has forced its way into our psyche, remapping our contentment substrate into an entitlement grid.

The particulars of the "escalation syndrome" dot every quadrant of our cultural map. I cannot think of a single instance—whether in celebrations, rituals, holidays, sports, cars, shopping, fashion, homes, commercial real estate—that has shown itself invulnerable to the pressures of escalation.

The following illustrations are but a few prominent examples of the syndrome. Please understand that I am not trying to embarrass any individual who has chosen this path of rising expectations, nor am I intending to invalidate the hard-working efforts of well-intentioned workers in any of these fields. But I am clearly intending to confront the intimidating cultural aristocracy that pushes the masses in this direction even against their better judgment. I wish to shine a light on exactly what is happening in this process, why it is happening, how our power to decide is diminished, and why we have the right to make these decisions—not by groupthink but for ourselves—according to our core priorities. That is, if we want our life balance back.

Homes, Vehicles, and Pets

It does not require a PhD in architecture to be aware of the escalation of the norm in housing. When the U.S. Census Bureau tracks the average square feet of floor space in new single-family homes, the trend is consistent: up.

In 1950, the average new home had 983 square feet of floor space, two bedrooms, one bathroom, and cost $11,000.

In 2000, a typical new home had 2,265 square feet, three or more bed-rooms, 2.5 bathrooms—plus a two-car garage, central air conditioner, one fireplace, and two stories—and cost $206,400.

In 2008, this had climbed to 2,534 square feet and cost $292,600.[6]

YEAR	SQ. FEET	AVG. COST
1950	983	$11,000
1970	1,500	$26,600
1990	2,080	$149,800
2000	2,265	$206,400
2008	2,534	$292,600

Not only have houses dramatically increased in size, but the number of occupants has decreased. This means that every person inside the home has three times as much floor space.

The luxury houses in the 5,000–8,000-square-foot category have also proliferated, and the rest of us drive through their neighborhoods and wonder what it would be like. The rooms are big, the ceilings are high, there are lots of windows, spacious foyers, huge staircases, three or four garages (sometimes called "garage mahals"), gourmet kitchens, sunrooms, walk-in closets, enormous master bedroom suites complete with whirl-pool tubs and separate showers, walk-in pantries in the kitchen, laundry rooms, media rooms, home offices, oversized garage doors (to accom-modate oversized vehicles), gas fireplaces, large decks—and, obviously, super-sized furniture.

Of course many celebrate this trend as a sign of our national prosper-ity. It's wonderful, perhaps, to have abundant space and to give each child his or her own room. It is one of the fruits of progress that is most con-spicuous and most gratefully received.

But there also is a price to be paid in our quest for balance. These larger homes—whether the 2,500-square-foot "average" kind or the 8,000-square-foot "McMansion" kind—have more space to clean and larger rooms to decorate, and then redecorate. Property taxes are higher, as are lawn care, utilities, assessments, and maintenance. The high mortgage costs require more work hours and often longer commutes—putting added pressure on dual wage-earners. The nights are shorter, the alarms sound earlier, and the kids are swept off to day care in the dark.

Vehicles have joined the parade. The huge SUV craze at the turn of the millennium saw expensive muscle cars in every driveway, with the Cadillac Escalade running as high as $85,000 and the Lincoln Navigator up to $60,000. Then there was the invasion of the Class A Super-Luxury RVs, "for those who want more." These behemoths stretch up to forty-five feet in length and cost as much as $3 million. Once they settle onto their campground landing strips, the expandable "side-outs" can be released along with the retractable awnings and the antennas for TV, radio, GPS, Wi-Fi, and weather monitoring.

Pets deserve a brief mention (I love them, by the way). Several sources list the need to buy your dog, for example, from a "reputable professional dealer" for $500 to $2,000. Plan on annual dog care to run $300 to $4,700 (double that in the first year), with the total lifetime spending between $4,000 and $71,000. Why so much? You will need high-quality food, treats, toys, beds, leashes, collars, fences, grooming, veterinary care, dental care, neutering/spaying, preventive medications and supplements, obedience classes, training, pet sitters, boarding, pet insurance, and emergency expense. And don't forget an occasional trip to the pet spa, plus prepaid cemeteries, crematoriums, and gravestones.

Is it not obvious how this relentless escalation of the norm has sabotaged our balance? To have a measure of simplicity in our "be it ever so humble" home will save time, effort, and money—plus give us a nice measure of equilibrium. What makes conspicuous consumers want to spend in these ways? Because they can! Well, actually, perhaps they can't. "Until the tide goes out," said Warren Buffett, "you don't know who is swimming naked." The economic tide went out, and many people, including the wealthy, are deeply embarrassed. The brutal collapse of the housing market brought foreclosures all across the spectrum, even in luxury homes. The $4.50/gallon gasoline prices resulted in millions of SUVs posting *For Sale* signs on the front window. And the dog? Well, perhaps we will keep the dog. It's always nice to have a friend.

Health Care

The story of healthcare escalation is epic, and it has brutalized untold millions of Americans, including workers within the system itself. This goes far beyond loss of balance and equilibrium, and spills over into the realm of confusion, frustration, anger, illness, and bankruptcy. It is a story in which everybody is to blame and nobody is to blame—except, of course, escalation. We can, with confidence, lay the blame there.

The healthcare debate has been raging for nearly two decades, and we are now in the midst of major change. Yes, in some ways, we have the best health system in the world. But it is also a deeply broken, unsustainable paradigm. Any futurist looking at the trends could easily predict that this moment would someday arrive. Only time will tell the final outcome, as it will take many years before the consequences of today's actions finish ricocheting throughout the system. The ideological and economic battles among interest groups will be both epic and interminable, and we can expect much weeping and gnashing of teeth from all sides. In the end, we will indeed have change, but there will most likely be one hundred million Americans who will be mad.

The largest problem, by far, is cost. It is not only the primary problem, but it drives many of the other collateral issues as well. We are spending $2.5 trillion per year on health care, which is 17 percent of our GDP. After mentioning this at a conference in Canada, someone asked me: "But the U.S. spends more on the military, doesn't it?" My response: "If we took all we spend on the military and all we spend on K–12 education, and added them together, and doubled it, then we would almost have the amount we spend for health care." What we have, in essence, is the largest, most expensive, and most complex domestic problem we have ever faced. All the simple problems were solved long ago—only the most difficult ones are left.

NATIONAL HEALTHCARE EXPENDITURES
Percent of Gross Domestic Product (GDP)

1960	5.2
1970	7.2
1980	9.1
1990	12.3
2000	13.8
2010	17.7
2020	20.1
2050	50.0

Why do these costs keep escalating so wildly and uncontrollably? If you want the short version, here's my one-sentence explanation: *There are more and more people living longer and longer with more and more chronic diseases taking more and more medications that are ever more expensive using more and more technology with higher and higher expectations in a context of more and more attorneys.*

The first half of this sentence speaks to positive developments in health care, and indeed in our society, that should be appropriately celebrated. There are *more and more people*—over 300 million now. That's not bad, it's good. Some of my best friends are people. We need a growing nation and a growing workforce in order to sustain our economy. *Living longer and longer*—this too is wonderful. Two thousand years ago, life expectancy was twenty-one years. In 1900, it was forty-seven years. Now it is seventy-eight years. This is magnificent. *With more and more chronic diseases*—over one hundred million Americans have chronic conditions that in the past would have killed them. We cannot cure these chronic diseases (such as diabetes, thyroid disorders, hypertension), but we can control them and keep the patient functioning for many years.

The second half of this sentence can be attacked. *More and more medications that are ever more expensive*—on the one hand, we know that modern medications work. They get people out of the hospital quicker, they keep them out of the hospital, and they keep them alive longer. But, on the other hand, they are outrageously expensive. *Using more and more technology*—many medical technologies are hyper-expensive and major drivers of escalating costs even though they are often of unproven benefit. *With higher and higher expectations*—patients frequently have unrealistic expectations, and there is much work to be done in this regard. If we ever hope to bring costs down, patients must lower expectations. *In a context of more and more attorneys*—tort reform for malpractice is essential. Personally, I've never been sued. But once a doctor receives that letter from the malpractice attorney and the suit makes the headlines, it will influence the treatment of every patient going forward in the direction of more protective—and more expensive—tests ordered.

I will resist giving my seven-hour lecture on healthcare reform and just summarize by saying that the escalation of the norm in medicine and health care is off the charts. It has become so out-of-control that, personally, I no longer trust any of the involved entities to behave responsibly in the cost debate—not hospitals, pharmaceutical companies, insurance companies, malpractice attorneys, physicians, patients, or the government. Yet each will be required to do its part if we are ever going to wrestle this monster into submission.

I drive past huge, beautiful new buildings for insurance companies, hospitals, and clinics and think, "Doesn't it occur to these people that the phrase 'cost containment' means 'trying to hold down costs'?" The unfathomable increase in expense seems to have little moderating effect on the way most of the system works. Why should we treat pharmaceutical manufacturers with appreciation when they charge $30 for a single migraine pill? Do you want to find out what a hospital or clinic procedure will cost? You can ask them, but they won't be able to tell you. It might be $1,000 or $10,000. You will not know until the bill arrives—and you might not know even then, because bills are often unintelligible. I once tried for days to unwind an invoice for a three-day hospital stay. Finally, I gave up in despair—and I'm a physician who has won math awards.

George Lundberg, the former editor of *JAMA* (*The Journal of the American Medical Association*) and a physician, once suggested in a continuing-education presentation that he removed his own seborrheic keratoses (those brown, bumpy skin lesions in older adults) with his fingernail. I think we might be headed back in that direction.

Weddings

"Weddings in Texas are a culturally-driven nightmare," wrote a friend caught in the midst of a matrimonial maelstrom. He loves his daughter and has enough money, but his frustration is palpable. "Of course this opinion does not make me very popular right now." Getting married has become hyper-expensive and sometimes hyper-competitive, increasingly driven by a pressure to conform to what others are doing. The ultimate humiliation, it seems, would be to have a substandard ceremony and reception.

I did a Google search on weddings and found that *wedding bride* registered thirty-one million sites while *wedding groom* came in at two million—perhaps that's why the bride's family pays? Beyond that . . .

Wedding gowns	40 million
Wedding songs	36 million
Wedding rings	33 million
Wedding flowers	31 million
Wedding cakes	28 million
Wedding invitations	21 million
Wedding reception	18 million
Wedding planners	11 million
Wedding planner fees	2.4 million
Wedding invitation wording	1.7 million
Wedding vows	1.6 million

Disconcerted that wedding vows—which I thought, perhaps naïvely, were the central part of the entire event—finished so low, I tried to give it cover by finding something beneath 1.6 million sites. First I tried wedding horses, but that was no help—6.2 million. Then wedding honeymoons— 7 million; wedding insurance—29 million; wedding manicures—1.7 million. At last, getting closer. But I still had to get below 1.6 million. I tried wedding guns—5.9 million. How about wedding semitrucks? 1.1 million. Finally.

The cost of an average wedding hit an all-time high of $28,000 in 2007 before dipping significantly with the recession. This sticker shock is highly stressful, and many feel trapped. They don't want to go into debt—many times they *can't* go into debt—but they also don't want the indignity of a "cheap" celebration. My question is, why did we ever allow such standards to take root in our culture? It is a complete falsehood—even approaching blasphemy—to say that an inexpensive wedding inherently lacks dignity. Some of the most undignified weddings I have ever seen have been very lavish affairs.

And then there is the time-consuming complexity of this escalation. It has been estimated that the average wedding takes over 250 hours to plan and organize. With the bride and groom often each working full time, they might have the interest to do planning but not the opportunity or energy. Thus the wedding planner. This might be an accommodation to necessity, but by adding another decision-maker, it also has the potential of additional considerations, choices, and cost. "Planning a wedding can be a stressful time, especially if all the details are disorganized," advises one service. "The last thing any couple wants to do is haggle over particulars and obsess over details." My first reaction was to think, "No, the last thing a couple wants to do is rack up stratospheric levels of debt equivalent to the down payment of a house."

Wedding planners have an answer for this. Yes, you pay for their services, but they have the ability to negotiate with caterers, florists, photographers, and other suppliers, have the time to shop around, and have the advantage of accessing discounts not available to private parties. All of this is true and perhaps important to consider. But obviously we have allowed such an escalation of the norm with weddings that as a consequence we need levels of bureaucracy and subspecialization to manage what otherwise could be a fairly simple ceremony.

It has been said that once you mention the word *wedding*, the price quadruples. The cost of a wedding photographer, for example, can run into the many thousands, and the accounting looks like this—high-quality cameras (as much as $30,000), lenses ($1,000 apiece), flashes, light monitors, tripods, camera bags, taxes, insurance, Internet postings, picture enhancement, printing, advertising, and assistants. Of course, newlyweds wish to have a beautiful photographic record of one of the most important days of their lives, and who can blame them? But soon they are swept along by a price momentum outside of their control.

And then there is the dress, the cake, and the flowers. The most expensive wedding dress in the world, valued at $12 million, is called the Diamond Wedding Gown, a 2006 Beverly Hills creation featuring 150 carats of diamonds. A 2009 Northeast China wedding witnessed the world's longest wedding dress train at 1.2 miles, which the groom's mother promptly called "a waste of money in my opinion." Then it's back to Beverly Hills for the world's most expensive wedding cake, bedecked with exclusive diamonds and jewels and valued at $20 million. Of course, the cake wasn't meant to be eaten or touched or, apparently, even seen, as it was surrounded by a team of armed guards. For the most expensive bouquet, we cross the Pacific again to that bastion of capitalism, Vietnam. This bouquet, valued at $125,000, has ninety gemstones, nine diamonds, and a star-shaped ruby and is on display at one of Hanoi's most sophisticated marketplaces, the Ruby Plaza, which "offers six levels of high-end retailers, a luxury day spa, and a rooftop bar restaurant."[7] The overall prize for most expensive wedding goes to London-based Indian-born steel tycoon Lakshmi Mittal on behalf of his daughter, Vanisha. For the 2004 wedding, Mittal, one of the richest men in the world, splashed $60 million around at several of Paris's most exclusive locations. One Indian magazine ran the headline "Papa, Buy Me the Eiffel."

People love to read of such affairs in the tabloids, but is there anything here to suggest these young couples will be any more happily married than the two farm kids being wed tomorrow in Bismarck? If it's long-term marital success we're talking about, I'll put my money on North Dakota every time.

I am not intending to suggest that the entire $33 billion wedding industry is populated by manipulative con artists who prey on vulnerable starry-eyed youth caught in the jowls of vicious cultural norms. Neither am I trying to deprive hard-working people the fruits of honest labor. But I am intending to suggest that if we wish our balance back by virtue of a sustainable economic lifestyle, the wedding is an appropriate place to make this first statement. Fifty or a hundred years ago, weddings were performed in the bride's church before "building-usage fees" had been invented. The groom wore a suit and the bride a dress she or a friend or relative sewed, or perhaps borrowed. The reception was cake, coffee, and punch in the church basement, and gifts were toasters, bedsheets, and card tables. Honeymoons were usually places you could drive within half a day. Yet, when the sun set—exactly as it inevitably does—they were just as married and just as happy.

But if our blissful young couple fifty or a hundred years ago was just as married and just as happy then, why exactly have we agreed to such a costly and coercive escalation of wedding practices? What is the benefit for us, given that we pay such a price in money and stress?

Of course, we are never going back to those earlier days. I understand and accept that. But even today, if a couple wished, they could get married for $800 in someone's front yard and ask the guests to bring a dish to pass. A $28,000 wedding does not get you any more married than an $800 wedding—it just raises your debt level. At the end of both events, the establishment of a legal union is precisely the same. The difference is that in the expensive wedding, you have the temporary approval of a culture that has one hand around your throat and the other hand around your wallet, while in the inexpensive wedding you have that aforementioned down payment for a house. Or a couple years of free rent, or the price of a new car, or two years of higher education at a state university, or perhaps you have paid off all your existing debt instead of multiplying it. The pastor at our wedding said all you really need to get married is a double bed and a frying pan—and I'm not so sure about the frying pan.

Again, please understand the point I'm attempting to make. I don't disapprove of wedding planners or photographers—I know several, and they are delightful people who take joy in serving the aspirations of excited young lovers. I'm not the least opposed to celebration—I *love* weddings and cry at every one. And I am not cynical about cakes and gowns and expensive rings. I just want to level the playing field, to give simple weddings a chance at equality, to erase the unfair cultural stigma against an inexpensive ceremony, and to wrestle the choice of wedding style away from a coerced societal bias and present it as a totally free choice to any newly engaged couple.

If we want balance back in our lives, we must be willing to confront the forces of escalation and coercion wherever they are found. If we fail to confront these forces in weddings—the complicated structures, the stressful expectations, the stratospheric expenses—newly engaged couples will simply opt out of the traditional church ceremony and instead tie the knot in a meadow or on a beach with a few close friends.

Funerals

There are approximately 2.4 million deaths in the United States every year—and that, regrettably, sounds like the beginning of a lucrative business model. The passage from this earth, whether sudden or slow, is accompanied by a lot of pressure on unprepared relatives who desperately want to honor the deceased while not simultaneously entombing their checkbooks. The rapid-fire logistical and financial decisions that follow are often complicated by rigid societal norms and expectations, to say nothing of state laws. As a result, instead of people doing what they really want to do, they end up doing what everyone else thinks they should do.

We live in one of the few times and locations in history that associates death with old age. All throughout the millennia and even in most countries today, death happens for any reason, at any time, and all along the age spectrum. As a result of this brutal reality, communities worldwide know exactly what to do with death—they hand it over to family, friends, faith, and tradition. In today's more affluent countries, however, we have institutionalized not only death but dying. We pay professionals to manage it for us, partly because it is painful, partly because it is unfamiliar, and to a large extent because it can be horribly messy. As a result, we pay a price—not only in dollars, but also a spiritual and relational price. Managing the details of passing ourselves can be a blessing rather than a burden and is perhaps the final gift given by the deceased to those who remain.

The average cost of a traditional funeral is between $6,000 and $12,000, including the services at the funeral home, the burial in a cemetery, and the installation of a headstone. But to be more precise, the differentiation of this ritual has become quite complicated and there are many variables to be considered: the funeral director's services, a casket, embalming, using the funeral home for the actual funeral service, a gravesite, digging the grave, a grave liner or outer burial container, a headstone, placing the obituary in the newspaper, flowers, limousine rental, prayer cards, use of the hearse, and a donation to the organist, soloist, or officiating clergy.

Many of these services and the associated costs are hidden inside the various "packages" offered by funeral homes. Unfortunately, the full breakdown of fees is often not revealed until the final bill. I am not the only one disturbed by a lack of full transparency in this matter, particularly when considering the grief of the bereaved, the mixed expectations among family members, the long-distance arrangements, and the lack of sensitivity to fragile bank accounts. I do not mean to be impugning the character of our many kindhearted morticians, but I am indeed determined to strike a blow for freedom whenever decision control has been taken away, particularly if by intimidation in a vulnerable setting. Our search for life balance is a difficult journey, and we must seek advantage wherever possible.

It is precisely these pinching issues that have led to a welcome democratization of the funeral activity. Aspects of the death and dying process are being redefined and renegotiated. Take cremation, for example. The rapidly rising rate of cremation now stands at about 35 percent for the nation (from the highest: Nevada, 65 percent; Washington and Hawaii, 64 percent; Oregon, 63 percent; Arizona, 60 percent; to the lowest: Kentucky, 12 percent; Tennessee, 11 percent; Mississippi and North Dakota, 10 percent),[8] and it is predicted to continue rising for the foreseeable future. While people have varying views on cremation from traditional and theological perspectives, the movement to embrace it has been noted in both the church and the wider public. I am not trying to convince anyone of the virtues of cremation. Instead, I'm only arguing for the restoration of balance against the escalation of the norm and pointing out that the increasingly popular choice of cremation is evidence of families reasserting their right to funeral self-determination.

There are many possible reasons for the cremation trend, but cost, simplicity, and flexibility are probably the most determinant. If the cost of a traditional funeral is $6,000 to $12,000, the cost of cremation following funeral service is $4,000 to $6,000, the cost of a cremation with a funeral home is $2,000 to $4,000, and the cost of a simple cremation with a crematorium is $1,000 to $3,000. Obviously, the savings in each case come from the lack of embalming, no purchase of a gravesite or headstone, no digging of the grave, no limousine and hearse, and minimized mortuary services in general.

Cremation is not the only option available to those wishing more choice in funeral costs. For purposes of comparisons, other choices—from least to most expensive—include (1) medical donation of the corpse, (2) direct cremation, (3) immediate burial, (4) cremation with a service, or (5) a traditional funeral.

There is another movement beginning to assert itself, called home-after-death care, where the body remains in the home until burial. This, too, is related not only to frugality and simplicity but also a more personal involvement with the deceased. In the intriguing Smithsonian article "The Surprising Satisfactions of a Home Funeral," Max Alexander relates the experience of losing both his father-in-law and his own father within seventeen days. Even though both were devout Catholics, the funeral choices were starkly different. Max's father, a politically conservative advertising man from Michigan, wanted a traditional funeral; Sarah's father, a left-wing journalist from Maine, wanted an inexpensive cremation. Honoring the wishes of her father to keep costs low, Sarah began investigating the home-after-death model while her father was in hospice with brain cancer. A few weeks prior to Bob's passing, Max and his son made a plywood casket for $90—inexpensive yes, yet lovingly designed, cut, assembled, stained, oiled, burnished, and topped with a cross of cherry on the lid.

When Bob passed, they were ready. Almost all states allow the body to remain in the home for at least twenty-four hours after death anyway, and if the intention is direct internment or cremation, no embalming is

ever required. In this case, following the death, with a deep sense of purpose Max and Sarah laid out his body in the living room and then washed
it with warm water and lavender oil. At first there was a bit of awkward
hesitation, but it quickly became second nature. Later that evening, they
brought the coffin into the living room, filled it with cedar chips (and
some freezer packs), lined it with a blanket, and placed Bob inside. The following evening they held a vigil, as family and friends streamed through
the living room to view Bob surrounded by flowers and candles. "He
looked unquestionably dead," said Max, "but he looked beautiful." The
next day he was cremated.[9]

Advocates of home-after-death care say it provides a more personal
and healing alternative to the institutionalized funeral home approach.
A case in the D.C. area involved the passing in his sleep of a ninety-one-
year-old man with Alzheimer's. The daughter and her family washed and
dressed the body in a process they said "felt very biblical." As he lay in the
guest room, friends and relatives started coming. "Some didn't want to go
up, which was fine. Some friends came and just sat there with him. We
kept a candle burning. It was so good. It was just quiet. We were kind of
seeing him out. It felt like we were really caring for him."[10]

Shortly after the turn of the last century, a hundred years ago, the wid-
owed Elinore Pruitt set out from Denver to ranch in Wyoming. There she
married her employer, Clyde Stewart. Elinore carried on a correspondence
with her Denver friend, and those letters resulted in the 1913 publication of a remarkable volume, *Letters of a Woman Homesteader.* Here is her
tender story of baby Jamie.

Do you remember, I wrote you of a little baby boy dying? That
was my own little Jamie, our first little son. For a long time my
heart was crushed. He was such a sweet, beautiful boy. I wanted
him so much. He died of erysipelas. I held him in my arms till the
last agony was over. Then I dressed the beautiful little body for the
grave. Clyde is a carpenter; so I wanted him to make the little coffin.
He did it every bit, and I lined and padded it, trimmed and covered
it. Not that we couldn't afford to buy one or that our neighbors were

not all that was kind and willing; but because it was a sad pleasure to do everything for our little first-born ourselves.

As there had been no physician to help, so there was no minister to comfort, and I could not bear to let our baby leave the world without leaving any message to a community that sadly needed it. His little message to us had been love, so I selected a chapter from John and we had a funeral service, at which all our neighbors for thirty miles around were present. So you see, our union is sealed by love and welded by a great sorrow.[11]

Restoring Balance by Resisting Escalation

Every choice we make in the direction of an escalation of the norm will lead to an erosion of our balance. If we are continuously reaching and redefining, we will be continuously disoriented. Our first job, then, is to decide what "normal" is.

Remember the statement from earlier in this chapter: "What we are witnessing is a continuous *escalation of the norm* followed rapidly by a *normalization of the escalation* that then becomes *the new normal*."

So, what *is* normal?

If, for you, "normal" is something bigger, something better, something more expensive, fancier, different, the next "new" thing—if that is normal for you, then you have made your choice. You have cast your lot with escalation and against balance. I won't pester you about it because I don't believe in force-feeding people who are not interested.

But if, for you, "normal" is whatever best serves your long-term priorities, then you have made a decision to be biased against escalation in favor of balance, sustainability, and priorities.

I am not speaking here of a boring constancy with absolutely no change. That's a silly idea, so impractical that it's laughable. That's like saying, "The hurricane is rocking this part of the boat, so let's go find a different place in the boat where it's not rocking." Anyone living in this era and in this culture is continuously being rocked by change. There is no avoiding it. We will all need to learn to keep our balance in stormy seas.

But there are two kinds of change—the good kind, and the not-so-good kind.

Positive Change—Change is necessary for growth. I not only agree with that statement, I thoroughly endorse it. But it must be the right kind of change. If we wish to grow and improve in the direction of our highest priorities, this will entail change. God, for example, has a huge change agenda for my life. I accept it without hesitation.

Negative Change—The culture, too, has a change agenda for my life. Ninety percent of these messages are suspect. Especially suspect are the messages that tempt us into believing that continuous escalation is a healthy process. It's about as healthy as weekly colonoscopies.

The change we embrace should be in the direction of our higher priorities. This is the kind of change that God speaks of, and it is the kind of change that leads not only to our growth and stability but also to our joy. Our deathbed already knows this lesson well.

Rx 1 Make Your Choice

I don't want to be redundant, but we need to understand that we are at a decision point here. Do you want escalation, or do you want balance? You can have the escalation of the norm, or you can have balance. But you can't have both, at least, not for very long.

You can keep eating the candy, or you can get your diabetes under control. At the end of the day, don't blame your doctor for your disease if you're still gulping a pound of chocolates before every sunset.

Rx 2 Develop a Bias for Function over Escalation

The vast majority of escalation of the norm is not only unnecessary but also probably destructive. Most Americans already have enough. By this I mean we have what we need. But we keep reaching up nevertheless, as if perhaps escalation might eventually unlock the gate into utopia.

What would happen if instead of reaching up, toward fashion, we reached over, toward function? Of course we'll take care to assure there's sufficient fashion to make things pleasing and attractive—that would not be difficult. But if 95 percent of our efforts went into optimizing function, what would the world look like? All products would be marked by durability, sturdiness, simplicity, and dependability. Parts would be easily replaceable. Costs would be low and widely affordable.

Take automobiles, for example. This year's models are sufficient—but that never stops us from looking over the fence to see how green the grass is under next year's models. So automakers build a new style because we want it, and we want a new style because they build it. I suspect we could long ago have chosen to perfect inexpensive, comfortable, functional automobiles with exceptional gas mileage, if all research and development across all automotive lines went into such a targeted functional goal. Such vehicles would not rust, and many repairs could be easily accomplished by individual owners.

Function is foundational, and it stabilizes balance. Fashion is not foundational, and it destabilizes balance.

Function has a destination—an improved product, for example. Fashion only has a temporary destination. Tomorrow, the destination will be different.

Function is measured objectively. Fashion does not follow an objective standard but instead is relative and comparative.

Because fashion is essentially insatiable, it leads to an ever escalating norm that never finally arrives. There is indeed a defense of the role of fashion that can be made—but not in the context of balance. Finally, on our deathbeds, fashion will be the last thing on our minds—at least, I hope so.

Rx 3   Consider Older Vehicles

For some, paying $25,000 for a new vehicle might be consistent with both their balance and their long-term priorities. For others, however, such an expenditure would do serious harm to their equilibrium. Fortunately we live in a country with millions of fine used cars, and, if you're good with the Internet, an easy source to find them. Our son Matt, while working in Indonesia, once bought a used Subaru in the Twin Cites via CarSoup.com. Matt spotted the ad, got his brother, Adam, to test-drive it, and twelve hours later, the car was his. It's been a wonderful addition to our family.

Personally, I've never spent more than $4,000 on a vehicle, and I don't feel a bit scarred by the experience. Quite the opposite—I feel I won. I beat the system. Not only does our family pay a relative fraction for car purchases but also for licensing, titling, taxes, and insurance.

The automobiles we buy look acceptable enough, and some are really quite nice. Often, you might never guess about the higher miles. There are times it's a bit awkward, though, such as when I'm speaking for a medical group at a country club. But I just arrive early and park under a big oak at the end of the parking lot. No biggie, as my granddaughter says. I'm not really embarrassed about the car; it's just that, like the geriatric of every species, sometimes they leak.

It's not that I'm virtuous; it's just that I'm cheap. I am a frugal utilitarian. My aim is to get from Point A to Point B in a timely, reliable, and inexpensive manner. Beyond that, I don't care. Last time I checked, my standing with God was still fine.

Rx 4 Stop Staring at the Neighbors

If we play the comparison game, we're sunk. No matter which direction we turn, we'll see people—our friends, neighbors, co-workers, fellow church-goers, even our family—running after escalation. And then we'll see them returning with a beaming countenance and a shiny new thingamajig in their hands—the kind no one else has yet. And we'll think, "That could be me." Be ready for it. If this triggers envy, our resolve might weaken.

Try refocusing. Instead of feeling envious, perhaps try being happy for their good fortune. This might be a gracious turn-of-phrase, but nevertheless, it's always winsome to rejoice with those who rejoice. Or, perhaps, try being mildly sad (not condescending) that they fell a bit short of their highest priorities on this occasion—as we all do. Or, best of all, stop noticing altogether. Stop wasting energy monitoring the lives of other people. Just focus on the road ahead. For us, home lies beyond the road ahead, and it is with a peculiar kind of joy that we engage the struggle to remain balanced and upright.

Rx 5   Don't Allow Others Power over Lifestyle Decisions

If we allow, culture will dictate our decisions and even live our lives for us—but not out of friendship. It's not easy finding the strength to resist the crowd, but balance will not be found in the default direction of the cultural treadmill.

Our culture has many layers of asymmetry. For example, it contains layer upon layer of asymmetrical power structures. We can often identify them by their extension of intimidation into the realm of our lives. For example, advertisers—they are easy to spot. They subtly make fun of people just like us, hoping that in embarrassment we will buy their products to escape the implied inferior status they've just identified us with. Or celebrities, the rich and famous. They, too, are easy to spot but mostly harmless. Their intimidation does not extend into our living rooms. We might envy them a bit, but we laugh at them even more, and they are no direct threat to our psyche. Or people in our area who have more wealth, better education, better looks, or a higher standing than we do. Some of these wield power in benign or even beneficent ways, and we do not fear them. We respect them and appreciate their efforts on behalf of the community. But then there is another category: those who make us feel uncomfortable whenever they are near. Why is that so? What do we fear? Their power to make us feel inferior.

I have no interest in any form of class warfare. I do, however, insist that people who've consciously made the decision to resist the escalation of the norm be allowed to freely live that choice in our midst without intimidation. If they live in simple housing, wear older clothes, or drive older cars, they are free to park next to any other car, especially, for example, in the church parking lot.

And a word to those who feel vulnerable. Whatever pressures you experience, choose to live by the brighter lights of heaven rather than the manipulations of darkened fears. "Learn from me, for I am gentle and humble in heart," Jesus said.[12] "Let your gentleness be evident to all," wrote the Apostle Paul.[13] "Kindness, I've discovered, is everything in life," said Isaac Bashevis Singer, Nobel laureate in literature. Confront power with gentleness, humility, and kindness. But do not bend and do not turn aside from your chosen direction.

Rx 6   See It, Name It

The more we know, the more we see. Once we "know" what to look for, we will "see" escalation everywhere—interstate rest areas, mattress sizes and comfort numbers, computer features, Internet devices, summer camps (etiquette camp, enuresis camp, stunt camp, weight loss camp, robotics camp, language camp, art camp, water polo camp, dance camp, atheist camp), coffee options at Starbucks (55,000), the size of fast food drinks (McDonald's first drink was five ounces; now its largest is forty-two ounces), motorcycle bling ("What counts—more bling/more bragging rights").

Psychiatrists teach that being able to name our enemy gives us a measure of power over it. The phenomenon of escalation is firmly entrenched in our collective psyche, and, make no mistake, it will be difficult to dislodge from our behavior patterns. But knowing what it is, and seeing where it is, brings understanding. And understanding is its own reward.

Rx 7   Resist the Escalation of Birthdays and Christmas

I love giving gifts to our granddaughter, Katja. Who wouldn't? But I am under no illusion that increasing the number and size of her gifts will actually make her a better girl, or a happier child, or a more successful person in life. Despite the complete absence of such proof, society has nevertheless escalated gift-giving for almost all occasions: birthdays, Christmases, weddings, bar mitzvahs, graduations, confirmations, first communions, first camping trips, first time to spot a spider outside the house. I know a couple who gave a new car when their only child got her first driver's license. (Guess what happened next?)

Sometimes we are embarrassed into gift escalation ourselves simply because the increasing norms have finally beaten us into submission. How do you give your cousin an embroidered pillowcase for Christmas when your cousin gives you a canopy bed?

Rx 8   Live from the Inside Out

In an informal discussion with a group of Mayo Clinic physicians, I mentioned my used-car philosophy. The story of my driving into the hospital parking lot and pulling up next to the British surgeon's luxury vehicle elicited smiles, especially the part about his three understated license plates: Rolls Royce 1, Rolls Royce 2, and Rolls Royce 3. Then one doctor commented: "You must have a lot of ego strength." It took me aback. I guess I've never thought of it that way. But it is true that if people attempt to live differently, they should be prepared for the cultural push-back. It is not always comfortable, and a reservoir of inner strength is important.

I guess in my own situation, I've always known that following my principles might be a bit awkward when those principles flow counter to the norm. Since I'm two standard deviations off the mean, I don't expect *Lifestyles of the Rich and Famous* to call for an interview. I virtually never make a fashion statement, and if you ever see me in trendy clothes gracing the cover of *GQ* magazine, you'll know it's a con, on the same level as the guy who faked his death and wrote his own obituary in an attempt to get off Harvard's mailing list.

We should feel free to disallow the world's opinion if we know that opinion is wrong. If we resist the tyranny of escalation when others don't, why should that make us feel insecure? Eleanor Roosevelt has gotten a lot of well-deserved mileage out of her classic observation: "Nobody can make you feel inferior without your consent." Perhaps the real issue is not "out there" but "in here." We can't control what others think or say. But we can keep them from setting up base camp inside our head, and we can control our own responses and internal dialogue. When we come home at night, get ready for bed, and finally turn out the light, that's when character shines the brightest. What is it that we know about ourselves in the dark?

It has been said that we live with two report cards—one on the outside and the other on the inside. Inner authenticity is infinitely more valuable than playing to the crowd. And since God only looks at the inside,[14] I've always thought that is the garden I should be tending.

Rx 9   Compare the Opportunity Cost

"Opportunity cost is a simple enough idea," writes Erik Richardson, an independent management consultant, "though overlooked on a surprisingly large scale. The basic principle is that whenever we spend money on one thing, we pass up the opportunity to spend it on something else . . . This works the same way for both time and money."[15]

For every choice we make, another possible course of action is lost to us. When it comes to the escalation of the norm, for every hour and dollar spent reaching up, we have lost the opportunity of using that time and money to stabilize our balance. For example, perhaps our automobile is running fine but the odometer indicates the need for an upgrade. We talk it over, look at the sales, shop around, visit dealerships, do some test-drives, and then write out the check. But this time might instead have been spent resting, or reading to the children, or visiting with our friends. And the money might have been used to pay down the mortgage or save for college.

Calculating opportunity cost can, at times, be complicated and almost paralyzing. Do we take the kids to the Grand Canyon, or do we build on to the family room? Do I leave my job for more education, or keep the job and try to begin our family? Do I watch the Cubs lose on TV, or do I floss my teeth for three hours? I know of one community-minded man who refused a traditional casket and funeral because of the opportunity cost. He specified cremation so he could give $6,000 to area children needing dental care.

I once received an email from a man in Seattle who wanted to tell me his story. He was offered an International Vice President position in the financial-services firm where he worked. As a part of his new responsibilities, he would be required to answer his BlackBerry within five minutes for any important message, 24 hours a day, 365 days a year. As he considered the honor of being selected and the generous compensation package, he also thought about his family. Finally, with his children's violin recitals playing in his head, he turned down the promotion. His balance would have been destroyed, and his time with the family would have suffered. The opportunity cost was just too high.

Life is a continuous series of trade-offs. "The distresses of choice are our chance to be blessed," said W. H. Auden.

Rx 10 *Resist Escalation of the Norm in Technology*

There is no "norm" in technology because technological development continues to advance at such a furious rate. Whenever we reach a decision point, that point is arbitrary. It cannot really be called the new normal, because as soon as the words pass our lips, a *newer* new normal has already come, and gone. It reminds me of the recently discovered strange subatomic particle neutral B meson that flips back and forth between itself and its own opposite antiparticle three trillion times a second.[16] The only difference is that tech changes just a wee bit faster.

If we wish to play this game with technology, it will keep us continuously destabilized. We cannot win. So we make our choices based on features, functionality, speed, and price . . . then return to real life.

Rx 11 Choose a House by Priorities

People who purchase large houses say they make such a choice "because we can." This may be an accurate phrase referring to financial resources, but it is also a little too flippant. Why, really, do we seek space in this way? The simple answer is that it's nice to have the room, to not be bumping into each other all the time, to give each person his or her needed space. It's also nice for purposes of hospitality. And, to be honest, it feels good to display our worldly successes. But on the downside, some rooms are so exquisitely appointed that no one goes in them. Other rooms become indoor storage sheds. The effort required to clean the place is extraordinary. And because of personal televisions, a family of four can now live alone together.

Why did Ronald Reagan like his 1,500-square-foot ranch house? Buffett's home is certainly larger, but still he has contentedly stayed put for fifty years. Our home for thirty years has 1,432 square feet. Yes, we have now improved half the basement, so that adds space. No, we are not planning to add on. Yes, we like it as it is. It's cozy, yet large enough to house people from Minnesota, Washington, Jamaica, and Nigeria for periods ranging from six months to five years. Paul, our remarkable African friend, turned to me during dinner and asked, "Why do people in America say they only have enough room for two children?" He looked around behind him. "In Africa, I could sleep twenty-five people in here." I had no answer for him.

So, enjoy your home, and God bless you. May it be filled with love and laughter. And may it recline beside you on your deathbed as a friend to your priorities and as a friend to the world.

Rx 12 Choose an Interior Redesign Endpoint

Deciding how far one should go in replacing household furniture, upgrading appliances, laying new carpet, and freshening the décor can be difficult, especially for those who love to redecorate. Some like to change often as a matter of preference and aesthetics; others change because of visible wear and tear; still others make changes only as a last resort.

The escalation of the norm has accelerated this schedule in all cases—those twin mattresses up to double, the double up to queen, the queen up to king, and the king gets a pillow top. But, as we have seen, every upgrade incurs an opportunity cost, depriving another possibility for that investment of time and money. It also perturbs our balance through the work of choosing new fabrics, colors, and styles, the stress of upheaval while the revisions are being done, and then the pressure of paying for it. Finally, there is the matter of our friends, who might feel slightly uneasy that perhaps now it's their turn to "keep up with the Joneses." Never forget that everything is connected to everything else—our actions have consequences.

Rx 13 Get a Million-Dollar Slum-Dog

Yes, we could go to a "reputable professional dealer" and buy a pet for $500 to $2,000 as discussed earlier. Or, on the other hand, we could drive to the pound and pick out a priceless border collie named Lassie. She quickly became a member of our family, and I told everyone she was not for sale. If you wrote me a million-dollar check, I would have torn it up.

We will never know why her previous owner beat her. She was a quiet, happy dog with a regal bearing. When she walked, she pranced like the princess she was. Everyone loved her for miles around. She could ride six hours in the car, curled up on the floor, and not make a peep. When she died, we buried her in the backyard and marked the grave with flagstones. Adam wrote a poem, "Companion," and read it bravely over her grave. Then he placed it in the hole next to her lifeless black-and-white frame. That was a dark day.

We are forever grateful that we didn't bow to the escalation of the norm, for we would never have met our sweet princess. She didn't ask for much, and we never spent much. She wasn't a classy dog, just the kind of dog every family dreams of owning.

Then came Reggie, followed by Sam. Both from reputable professional dealers. If you had shown up on the right day with a shiny quarter, you could have had them both.

Rx 14 Don't Allow Culture to Determine Wedding Spending

There are dozens of decision points in a wedding. The ring, for example. The average amount spent on a diamond engagement ring is $1,000 to $4,000, and if the decision is freely made, I have no desire to interfere. But our culture has assigned a "value" to this that is far different than the "with this ring I thee wed" vow, and instead is about cultural approval. I submit to you that the one has nothing to do with the other. They might indeed coincide, but they can also be as divergent as Neptune and a cheeseburger.

Linda and I discussed this upon our own engagement in 1970 and without any stress decided on the Swedish custom of two plain gold bands—one for the engagement and the second for the wedding. Our son and his lovely new wife, who both do aid work in difficult and impoverished countries, gladly exchanged the same rings Matt's grandparents used. May they symbolize as much faithfulness and joy in the second union as they did in the first.

If you have the time to plan, the creativity to be innovative, and the strength to resist pressure, you can design an exceedingly dignified and spiritually centered wedding for a fraction of the national average. And who knows, maybe you will even start a trend.

Rx 15 Take Back Your Funeral

It is your life, it is your death, and it is your funeral—begin planning it now. I have been doing so for over a decade and have, for example, chosen four songs that I wish to be used in the ceremony. I want a very simple ceremony celebrating people, faith, and joy. It is not morbid to think on such things but rather the most natural approach I can imagine. It also keeps my daily focus on appropriate deathbed priorities.

By working through details well in advance, an individual can, together with the family, decide on nearly every aspect of the ceremony including location, methods, costs, caskets, embalming, internment versus cremation, viewing, music, Scriptures, order of service, and participation. Look around at the various funeral homes and compare prices. Don't automatically accept the "packaged" options unless you know exactly what this entails and the associated fees. If the desire is to hold down costs, it helps when the deceased has given explicit permission in advance.

Don't feel guilty. Don't allow critical onlookers or the funeral home to take advantage of your vulnerability. Disregard the escalation of the norm with its rigidity and tremendous cost increases. If you desire simplicity and frugality, build your own casket, or forego embalming, or skip the limos, or consolidate the visitation and funeral service. Most importantly, abide by the wishes and sentiments of the deceased, as well as your own.

Rx 16 *Plan for the Casket of Your Choice*

Select your own casket preference, not the one thrust upon you. If it can be done in advance, all the better. Decisions made quickly under pressure often cost more than those made in advance. Remember Murphy's Law of Thermodynamics: *Things get worse under pressure.* Consider building your own casket, ordering one online (the funeral-home markup for caskets is two to seven times the factory cost), or obtaining an inexpensive plain one and decorating it to reflect the deceased's life and passions. Or, if you wish, choose the nicest casket money can buy.

My brother-in-law had a fur-trade museum on the North Shore of Lake Superior and always said he was born 300 years too late. He knew everything there was to know about the French fur-trading era. When he died prematurely of idiopathic pulmonary fibrosis at age fifty-one, his sons built his coffin, and we all marched out to Louis Armstrong singing "What a Wonderful World." Later, at the gravesite, his rendezvous friends gave him a ten-musket salute facing the largest freshwater lake in the world.

Personally, I have a strong preference for a simple casket, preferably homemade, similar to my brother-in-law's. I might even make it myself with, no doubt, a smile on my face since I'm a horrible carpenter. No matter, it's only a single crossing.

Rx 17 *Plan for the Light*

Finally, there is the matter of eternity—don't forget to plan for that. As for myself, I've been anticipating it for decades. When the gates swing open and the great light of heaven—what the Bible calls an "unapproachable light"[17]—comes pouring out, it will be blinding. Yet, somehow, I'll be able to see perfectly. As a Christian with training in physics, I can't wait to experience this phenomenon. And, beyond light, there is the glory of God, which is light to be sure but also something more—I suspect light combined with love.[18] It will be devastatingly beautiful. I'll never recover. Being surrounded by such infinite perfection would be awkward were it not for the welcoming presence of Jesus. One might think that those "rich wounds, yet visible above"[19] would make me cringe. But I know it's not necessary—He's not mad at me, not even when He first climbed out of the grave. He made peace with me, and then I was able to do the same with Him. We're friends.[20] So now, finally, my tiny portion of the great drama of eternity will be over. I will be home and, at last, will enter my rest.

7

DOING THE MATH

RICK MORANIS IS good at math. The comedic actor of such movies as *Honey, I Shrunk the Kids, Ghostbusters*, and dozens more, wrote an op-ed piece titled "My Days Are Numbered."

> I have five television sets. I have two DVR boxes, three DVD players, two VHS machines and four stereos. I have nineteen remote controls. I have three computers, four printers and two non-working faxes. I have three phone lines, three cell phones and two answering machines.
>
> I have no messages.
>
> I have forty-six cookbooks. I have sixty-eight takeout menus from four restaurants. I have three hundred and eight-two dishes, bowls, cups, saucers, mugs and glasses.
>
> I eat over the sink.
>
> I have thirty-nine pairs of golf, tennis, squash, running, walking, hiking, casual and formal shoes, ice skates and rollerblades.
>
> I'm wearing slippers.
>
> I read three dailies, four weeklies, five monthlies . . . I have five hundred and six CD, cassette, vinyl and eight-track recordings.
>
> I listen to the same radio station all day.[1]

We can learn a few things from Moranis's math. First, often it's the simple things we enjoy most. The things that we feel comfortable with, that we keep going back to, that we find reliable. Second, escalation and profusion came to us as improvements, but sometimes they just feel like clutter.

We would understand these things—and many more—if we just did the math.

Not Good at Math

Some people are not very good at math. Like Jon, who bought a $23 quadrillion meal at Wolfgang Puck's restaurant in north Texas. You'd think that somebody at Visa should have stopped Jon from spending more money than exists in the entire universe, particularly when using a prepaid charge card. But perhaps the $116 million per second of interest was too tempting.

Or, some Russian officials in the Volga region. They're also not very good at math. They "undervalued" four MiG-31 fighter-jet fuselages, worth $3.7 million each, on a list of sale items. As a result, prosecutors say, "long-range supersonic interceptor aircraft that were not for sale were purchased by a dummy firm"[2] for as little as $5 apiece.

Or, hockey player Patrick Kane, the twenty-year-old millionaire NHL star. He and his cousin James were arrested for assaulting a sixty-year-old taxi driver at 5:00 a.m. because the cabbie didn't have twenty cents change. Patrick made $3.725 million last year.

Or, the journalist who reported the FDA was considering requiring the 500 mg extra-strength acetaminophen be available by prescription only. That way, said the reporter, no one could take 1,000 mg without a doctor's Rx. (Unless, of course, they took three over-the-counter 325 mg pills.)

Or, John Bachar. But John is different. Unlike our other examples, John had a mathematics background. He studied it at UCLA, where his father was a mathematics professor. He was always rigorously analytical. He studied technique, balance, and strength. He calculated his every move.

So John was actually very good at math, and balance too. Except when it mattered most.

Born in Los Angeles, he was a passionate young man, first excelling in pole-vaulting at the elite Santa Monica Track Club and later transferring his skills to the mountains. As his love for the rocks became an addiction, he abandoned his studies at UCLA to give himself to the cliffs. Determined to be the world's best, in the 1970s he moved into Camp IV, a California hangout for seriously edgy rock climbers and an epicenter for devotion and daredevilry. John distinguished himself early because of his athleticism, his rigorous training program, his unmatched physique, his mental toughness, and his willingness to take breathtaking risks.

More than anything, it was his uncompromising adherence to free-climbing that made him world famous. Free-climbing—also known as free-soloing—is a pure, yet very dangerous, technique of ascending rocks and cliffs from the ground up without the use of any equipment—no ropes, no bolts, no safety net of any kind. "It was always breathtaking to see John gliding effortlessly upward on tiny knobs or with only the first knuckles of his fingers in a crack 100 feet off the ground," said climbing photographer Phil Bard. "It took superior training and complete control over his mindset to accomplish what he did."[3]

He scaled some of the most terrifying and treacherous formations in the West, many previously thought unclimbable even with equipment. Methodical, shrewdly calculating, graceful, pure, unhurried, unforced, artistic, anachronistic, stubborn, gloriously reckless—he was all these and more. In 1981 he offered $10,000 to anyone who could follow him for a day. No one was that good, or that foolish. Some of his fellow climbers were irritated by the one-upsmanship.

While night-driving through Nevada in 2006, he rolled his car, resulting in the tragic death of his business partner, Steve Karafa. Bachar himself suffered five fractured vertebrae. After surgery and a fusion, he never completely regained his once-stunning full mobility. Yet he returned to climbing while still wearing a neck brace.

On July 5, 2009, he fell unwitnessed while free-soloing at Dike Wall, a beautiful cliff of pristine granite in Mammoth Lakes, California. He died at age fifty-two, leaving behind a son, Tyrus, age twelve, who lived with him.

So, simplistically speaking, John Bachar was good in "theoretical" mathematics and perhaps in "analytical" mathematics. His analytical skills served him well for decades. But in the end, his failure was in "applied" mathematics. He'd said that his first safety tip was to give up free-climbing.[4] He never took his own advice.

Bachar was bad at math because in the end, gravity wins. Gravity always wins. Although it is by far the weakest of the four fundamental forces of physics, gravity has an infinite reach and thus rules the universe. That Bachar would fall, however, was not so much a matter of physics—it was a matter of mathematics. Ascending precipitous slippery cliffs without safety precautions is universally acknowledged to be a dangerous business. The very best climbers can do it once, or five times, or for a season, or for a decade. But they cannot do it at age ninety. Sooner or later, the declining competencies of an aging body can no longer match the relentless power of gravity. Every year, the probability of death increases. Eventually, if he didn't come down off the mountain, John was going to die.

In the end, we all must bow to the math.

Good at Math, Good at Balance

Math is our friend. If we apply it wisely, it will help us in life. It will keep us balanced, for example, in our time and finances. In fact, good math will help keep us balanced in all our expenditures of energy and resources.

But if we ignore the math, it will not ignore us. If we think we are smarter than the math, we will discover that, actually, the math is much smarter than we are. The math is always right. It does not lie. We might get away with neglecting the math for a while, but if we don't mend our ways, we will fall off a cliff.

So, with regard to balance, math is either our ally or our enemy. If the math is in balance, our lives will most likely be balanced also. But if the math is out of balance, our lives will stagger and slip and fall.

One of the reasons that math assumes an important role in any discussion of balance is because it helps us understand the forces arrayed against each other. When we assess the struggle between balance and imbalance, it's helpful to know what each side brings to the table. On the face of it, this looks quite simple. Why such a tussle? Why can't balance just stand its ground and hold firm? What kind of wind keeps blowing it over? Why, when we have so much progress, so many time-saving technologies and labor-saving devices, so much affluence and education, why can't balance just dig in like the Washington Monument?

One would think this might be the very best of times for balance, the time in all of history when balance would be most easily achieved and most readily sustained. Instead, the opposite seems true. What's going on?

The answer is that we live in mathematically epic times. The calculus has been destabilized. It has been said that "seldom do people realize the historic when they're living through it."[5] That's us. But if we wish, math will help us "realize the historic." Math will explain the nature of this titanic, almost irreconcilable, clash going on between balance and imbalance.

On the one side of the equation, we have *more and more of everything faster and faster*. As we will remember, this is the automatic result of progress. We don't even have to request it—it just comes. Not only is it automatic, but it also is dynamic. It changes continuously and rapidly, always ascending, always more. And no matter what we do, it just won't stop growing. It is one of the most powerful forces on the face of the earth today.

On the other side of the equation, we have our relatively fixed limits: time, money, physical energy, emotional resilience, intellectual capacity. We don't have to request these things either. They just automatically show up, a part of God's creation wisdom. These limits are not dynamic—just the opposite. They are static, at least relatively so. They stay the same. They change little. And no matter what we do, they just won't grow.

This equation explains the essence of our modern balance problem, and it is fairly simple to understand. We live right now at the interface of the two sides of this equation. When one side of the equation hits the other side, it yields a mighty explosion. Right now, on our generational shift, the fight has matured. Something has to give. When a 9.3 quake hits San Francisco, the buildings either stand or fall.

On the one side, the side of "more," we have a phenomenon that grows and doubles and expands and escalates. On the other side, the side of "limits," we have a phenomenon that sits like the Rock of Gibraltar. It is up to us to find a mathematical way to reconcile the one side to the other—because neither side is going to stop. Neither side can change its essential character. In the end, this is a mathematical problem. And unless we can reconcile the two sides of this equation *in our personal lives*, we will have increasing imbalance and dysfunction.

I personally think the equation is easy to grasp, but few seem to comprehend its implications. I've taught this to countless audiences, yet I often wonder how many "get" it. Some, perhaps, just don't like equations or mathematics. Some prefer to ignore trends until after the crisis. Some think, "Well, that's true for the next guy but not for me," when, in fact, there are no exemptions. Some are so driven they refuse to be told what they can and cannot do—fine, go ahead and climb the 500-foot cliff without a rope.

And then there are those who say this equation isn't true because we *can* change our limits. Finally, we have a discussion. I'm glad you brought it up, because you're right—we *can* change our limits. Just not very much.

To understand this better, let's break the discussion of our limits into two categories: societal limits and individual limits.

Societal Limits—Society is a system, and all systems have limits. However, society can expand its limits in various ways, and it does so all the time. Using technology, for example, society can learn to work faster, work longer (24 hours a day, 365 days a year), work smarter with more productivity, and work cheaper. Even given this expansion ability, however, society still is dangerously impinging on its limits and must learn to be more careful. In the management of such areas as our economic system, our healthcare costs, our federal budget deficits, our entitlement programs such as Medicare and Social Security, and even our demographics, society finds itself in serious difficulty because it has failed to respect its limits and the need for societal balance.

Individual Limits—Individual limits are much more constrained. We find that we can grow and adapt, take classes, discipline ourselves, develop more personal efficiencies, but still, the limits remain. For the most part, they are relatively nonnegotiable. We can only have so many thoughts. We can only say so many words. We can only make so many decisions. We can only tolerate so many interruptions. We can only see so many patients. We can only read so many articles. We can only focus on so many things.

And we do not multitask well.

Personally, I don't kick against it too much. God made us this way, and I try never to insult His creation wisdom. Everything I need to achieve in life can be achieved within the constraints I've been given. Our greatest accomplishments come not from ourselves anyway but from God working in us. And God has no limits.

Let's take time, for example. Time does not change.[6] Every year we each have 31,536,000 seconds. Everyone on the earth has exactly the same amount. It is not as if the wealthy get ten million seconds more than the poor. Nor do those with a college education get ten million seconds more than the uneducated. We all get exactly the same. The rich can buy a kidney from the poor, but they cannot buy time from anyone.

Some people think they can play with this number. They seem to believe that if they are particularly clever and if they challenge the gods, if they yell and scream and flex their muscles, if they blow smoke out of their ears and intimidate their surroundings, then next year they will get 35 million seconds rather than 31,536,000 million. Inevitably they are annoyed when it doesn't work. Bad math never works.

What happens when we try to ignore the math and believe the fiction that next year we'll squeeze more than 31,536,000 million seconds into our schedule? What happens when we pretend that reality will be suspended for us because we moderns are masters of the universe and nothing can stop us from getting what we want? First, we schedule ourselves in impossibly busy ways, adding 20 percent more responsibilities than the year before. Then when reality hits, we rush, shorten our sleep, multitask, take unacceptable shortcuts, compromise quality, shortchange relationships, take risks, become stressed out, and quit caring.

Money, too, is relatively fixed. We might, of course, get a raise or a pay cut, increasing or lowering our income perhaps 5 percent in a year. There are exceptions to this, of course, but I'm attempting to speak to the practical realities of most people's lives. The amount we live on, in the vast majority of cases, does not go from $30,000 to $60,000 to $20,000 to $120,000 in a four-year span. Most years, our income remains within a fairly predictable range. What happens if we make $44,000 one year and then decide next year to spend $55,000? There will be imbalance and there will be pain.

The same principle applies to physical energy, emotional resilience, and intellectual capacity. Yes, these can change, but again, usually not much—seldom more than 5 to 10 percent in a year.

Of course there are exceptions to what I have just said. We can get more out of our time by delegating, by using technologies and computers, by learning efficiencies, by eliminating time-wasting activities. All that is true. But on a personal individual level, we still have exactly 31,536,000 million seconds per year.

For those of us who trust in transcendence, this equation does not threaten us in the least. It has never been about my time, my energy, my accomplishment, my productivity. The multiplication coefficient for my power is the power of the Spirit of God.

Restoring Balance by Doing the Math

Our difficulty in recovering balance and then sustaining what we have recovered is that imbalance is not a single-point-source problem. Everywhere we look, we see the battle lines. Browse through a magazine, turn on your television, visit the hospital, open your refrigerator, boot up a computer, stroll through a Wal-Mart, lift the hood of your car. Or, skip all that and just pick up an appliance manual for a toaster. We are surrounded, continuously, by differentiation, proliferation, profusion, and escalation.

This does not annoy me, really. It just makes it a fair fight. God clearly is rooting for love, joy, peace, patience, kindness, goodness, faithfulness, gentleness, and self-control[7]—and the best context for these fruits is a balanced life. In which garden does this crop best grow? A field characterized by calmness, steadfastness, tranquility, serenity, and moderation? Or a field full of work dread, irritability, frustration, disorganization, exhaustion, and burnout? There is much at stake, and the topic extends far beyond pop psychology.

Because the fight is broadly scattered, we will use every advantage available. I have already stated repeatedly that math is on our side, and this is true diagnostically and therapeutically. If the math harmonizes, all is well. But if the math is off, our balance will be off. If the math doesn't work, our balance won't work. If the math is messy, our balance will be messy.

Following are many prescriptions for balance using some loose formulations of mathematics. Math will tell us helpful truths and hurtful truths, but always the truth. Learn to do the math, and learn to trust the math. It points the way.

Rx 1   Do the Math on Schedules

To be mathematically rigid about schedules might work for some, but it is not the right approach for most. Yet even if we dispense with the rigidity, we ought not throw away the mathematics. We each have 86,400 seconds per day. If we schedule ourselves for 90,000 seconds per day—an extra hour—the reality will not yield to our fiction. As a result, we double-book, we skip lunch, and we get home after the kids are in bed.

One lady was endlessly complaining about her onerous schedule when finally a co-worker tired of the whining. Interrupting, she said, "But you schedule yourself!" If we let math be a friend of our schedules, we will get balance thrown in free of charge. We might make a bit less, but we will smile a lot more. Plan realistically. Build some margin into the schedule, a buffer, a short coffee break for the soul.

Rx 2   Do the Math on To-Do Lists

Every morning we gird up our loins and go to work on the world's problem pile. At the end of the day, hopefully, we can point to some accomplishments. The next morning, out we go again, only to find the same number of problems. So we dutifully check off each item on our to-do list and then go to back to bed secure. The next day, we have another to-do list, and it's just as long. We solve a problem in Quadrant A, but then a problem crops up in Quadrant B. So we solve the problem in Quadrant B, and a problem arises in Quadrant C. We solve problem #5, then problem #50, then problem #500. Shortly thereafter, problem #501 calls out for us.

I am a good problem solver. In the University of Wisconsin Family Practice residency where I worked, I solved problems every day. Yet after fifteen years, I had just as many problems to solve as I did before I started solving problems. And the residents were just as unhappy as they were before I started fixing problems.

This is not meant to suggest that we stop solving problems. But it is to suggest that we can run ourselves into the ground trying to whittle down our to-do list. I've come to realize that my main purpose on earth is not so much to be a problem solver as to be a lover of problem bearers. In medicine, for example, the 10:45 a.m. patient has a sore throat. We can treat the strep infection, but we also have the brief opportunity to love the patient. In ten days, the penicillin will be gone. But love remains forever.

Rx 3   Do the Math on Yes and No

No, for most of us, is an almost impossible word. It triggers a crisis of guilt and conscience—we'll disappoint our friends, we'll miss out, we'll not get promoted, others will think us weak, we'll be accused of selfishness. But whatever else it is, "no" is a simple mathematical concept. We are allowed by God to commit our "yes" up to twenty-four hours a day. After that, we must say no. This means, obviously, that if we have thirty hours of things to choose from on any given day, we will need to say no to six hours worth of activity, opportunity, entertainment, commitment, and obligation.

It's always been easy to say no to bad things, like hiking Death Valley, climbing K2 in bare feet, or cleaning the toilets at Leavenworth. But compounding the problem, so many of our choices today are enjoyable experiences, profitable opportunities, or social activities. How do we decide? At times, it can be paralyzing.

First, consult your deathbed. This is the advice you'll receive: "When you get up in the morning, what is it you *wish to do* today? And one hundred years from now, what is it *you'll wish you would have done today*? Do the latter." This speaks to timeless priorities, and it is always the correct course of action.

If we wish to have the time and energy for balance and for our highest priorities, the word *no* will be a useful tool. It is a powerful, holy word, one that Jesus said often. Use it well, and we will be blessed. But if we use it wrongly, our lives will be a disaster.

Rx 4   *Do the Math on Discretionary Burdens*

Canadian consultant Pat Katz provides an insightful weekly newsletter called PAUSE. As you might guess, the name speaks for itself. A year ago, she discussed the topic of discretionary burdens.

> It was late in the evening just before Hallowe'en. I was chatting on the phone with my daughter and had just recited the litany of tasks tackled so far that day . . . demanding day in the office . . . exercise class . . . running several errands on the way home . . . getting things ready around the house to host a guest for the weekend.
>
> As I finished giving report on my day, I heard myself say, "And I still HAVE TO carve the pumpkin before I can go to bed." Wise offspring played back my very own words. "You HAVE TO carve the pumpkin?" I could hear the raised eyebrow in her voice. And in that moment, I realized I'd just loaded myself down with yet another DB—a Discretionary Burden . . . Each task that we peg as an obligation adds to our feelings of overload. Those tasks approached in the willing spirit of service have an entirely different impact . . . The fewer tasks you tag as DB's, the lighter your load will be.[8]

That's a valuable lesson in itself, but with Pat's permission, I'd like to create a second application. Every day we fill our lives with things to do that weigh nothing on the scales of eternity. These discretionary burdens will be conspicuously absent on our deathbed. We say, "I have to wax the car, wet mop the garage floor, get a pedicure, watch *Dancing with the Stars*, renew *Postcard Collector Magazine*, fix the scratch on the front door, deworm the dog, and trim the bushes." Actually, we don't. These are purely discretionary. In 1850, no one thought of spending time on any of these. Each discretionary burden represents a tiny assault on our balance. But when taken together over a lifetime, they become a sledgehammer to the cerebellum.

Rx 5   Do the Math on Interruptions

If the first decade is any indication, the twenty-first century will be one of continuous interruption. Of course we've always had unanticipated situations, work stoppages, children needing help, and people calling out our names. But technology has raised the experience to a rousing—and untenable—level.

Depending on our personal situation and individual circumstances, we are interrupted between 20 and 200 times a day. Since our brain does not multitask well, we slow or stop what we are doing and turn to the source of the diversion. Our attention is sidetracked. In one Microsoft study of computer workers, when the interruption occurred in the form of a conversation, an average of sixteen minutes passed before renewed activity was seen on the computer.[9] Combine that with being interrupted sixty or one hundred times a day, and you have a workplace disaster.

Eighty percent of interruptions are for non-urgent matters, often social in nature. Sometimes we enjoy these breaks from our routines. We are pleased when the phone rings, the doorbell chimes, or a new email arrives with a tone. But on the other hand, whether at home or work, these intrusions can be a major challenge. "Every e-mail interruption is like a hand grenade being thrown in the middle of your brain," says psychiatrist Ned Hallowell, MD, author of the book *CrazyBusy*.[10] For those matters requiring sustainable effort, evenness, and efficiency, we must develop a new social etiquette that acknowledges the brutality of this unprecedented reality. We have, after all, the right to establish and defend the atmosphere in our own homes. And in our place of work, we have the responsibility of accomplishment on behalf of the person paying our wage. The entire society will simply need to change the unrealistic expectation of reaching anybody anywhere anytime instantly. There is no other mathematical choice.

Unapologetically and proactively restore a sense of control. Preempt disruptions in advance. Interruptions coming to us by way of technology require our permission—we own the technology; it does not own us. Turn it off. Or don't answer—I frequently don't. Don't admit you are present. Consider batching messages and emails, answering twice a day. Have phone calls routed to voice mail. Delegate this responsibility if possible. On occasion it will be necessary not to answer personal emails that arrive unsolicited. Or, perhaps simply state in a short message that you are unavailable. Be gracious, but firm.

When writing a book, I either write nights and sleep days or go away to a secluded place. I must have deep consecutive thoughts. When people are informed in advance, they have been uniformly cooperative. For that I owe you my gratitude.

Rx 6   Do the Math on Clutter

Clutter experts—and with home-organization solutions being a $7 billion industry, there are many such experts—offer us the 80/20 principle. This rule maintains that 80 percent of what we use comes from 20 percent of what we own.

If this is true—and it seems about right to me—the math is pretty compelling. The vast majority of what we own is never used. It is, however, stored, stacked, piled, cornered, shelved, boxed, searched through, stepped on, walked around, and at least minimally maintained. And every piece takes a nibble out of our balance.

Is it any wonder that in the era of profusion and escalation we should all be buried under piles of unused stuff? The frustration of clutter even reaches the Internet. One-third of users will immediately leave a site that is cluttered with ads.

We all have our weaknesses, and no one is suggesting this is a simple problem. But if clutter blocks our path and hinders our equilibrium, give it away or throw it out. And if all else fails, hire a bulldozer.

Rx 7   Do the Math on Wardrobe Choices

The 80/20 principle applies to our wardrobe as well. This means that more than three-fourths of the clothes in our drawers and closets go unused—but take up space anyway. Time, attention, and energy are spent maintaining things that are never, or at least very seldom, used.

Let's look at the math from a different angle. If we have fifty pieces of clothing to choose from every day, it will obviously take longer to get dressed than if we had five things to choose from.

Even if people dislike the conclusions, still the math is straightforward. Simplifying our wardrobe would make balance easier. In most cases, we could significantly debulk our closets, and our friends would never even know. Or, to be seriously cool, you could wear the same thing every day like Johnny Cash, Steve Jobs, or Albert Einstein.

Rx 8   Do the Math on House Size

We have already seen how home sizes have mushroomed over the past fifty years, from 983 square feet in 1950 to 2,534 square feet in 2008. There are both positive and negative considerations here, along with mathematical consequences for our balance.

On the positive side, a larger house permits the advantages of space, utility, privacy, hospitality, and a certain feeling of personal success. Plus, extra bathrooms, the benefits of which are backed up by centuries of sociological observation.

On the negative side, we have at least two mathematical consequences to ponder regarding balance. First, larger houses require larger mortgages; mortgages are paid with money; and money is given us in exchange for our time. It is therefore accurate to say that we pay a price for our larger homes that can be measured in years. Second, the larger the house, the longer the time to clean it. In each consequence, a larger home requires more time.

For some, this makes little difference. They have stable jobs, make plenty of money, and can afford cleaning help. For them, balance is not harmed. But many others sit in a middle zone. The math works, but it's tight. Painful trade-offs are required, some not consistent with long-term priorities.

Gauge the monthly pressure and the priorities, and then make your decision. Just be sure you're honest about the math.

Rx 9   Do the Math on TV

Are you ready for this? The average American now watches 153 hours of television per month, or five hours per day—an all-time high.[11] Why the increase? (1) The average home has more televisions than people. (2) There are many more niche cable channels. (3) Television watching is now time-shifted with DVR and TiVo devices.[12] At minimum wage, the total value of Americans' time watching television is $1.80 trillion per year.[13]

Might I be permitted a speculation: If all the televisions disappeared from the earth tomorrow, might 75 percent of all our balance problems be solved?

In 63 percent of households, the TV is "usually" on during meals. Sixty-eight percent of eight- to eighteen-year-olds have a TV in their bedrooms. Kids with a TV in their bedroom spend almost one and a half hours more per day watching television than kids without a set in their rooms. All television programming, even educational non-commercial programming, *replaces* physical activity in a child's life, and while watching TV, the metabolic rate seems to go *even lower* than during rest.[14]

Yes, there are significant positives about watching television. But if we want balanced lives for ourselves and our families, this is a good place to start. We shouldn't ever complain, "I have no time," if we are watching five hours of TV per day. Do the math.

Rx 10   Do the Math on Email

I love email. It is hard to imagine how I could function without it, especially given my dislike of telephones. But I also hate email. It is one of the biggest stressors in my life. It's all a matter of the math.

If a person receives one email per day, the volume is simple. If a person receives 500 emails per day, the volume is impossible. Somewhere in between is an optimal range. But, of course, as with everything, email escalates. It's difficult to make it behave.

Worldwide there were 247 billion emails per day in 2009, which is three *million per second*. Sixty-three percent of these were consumers and 37 percent were business. This is projected to double by 2013.

EMAIL VOLUME, DAILY WORLDWIDE[15]
210 b in 2008

247 b in 2009

294 b in 2010

349 b in 2011

419 b in 2012

507 b in 2013

Eighty-one percent of the total email traffic is spam, which equals 200 billion every day. For comparison, this was:

VOLUME OF SPAM, DAILY WORLDWIDE[16]
2 b in 2002

11 b in 2004

30 b in 2005

55 b in 2006

100 b in 2007

200 b in 2009

The typical corporate users send and receive about 167 messages daily and will spend 30 percent of their day creating, organizing, reading, and responding to email.[17] Businesses wishing to store all these messages need to allocate 20 MB of storage space per user per day. Organizations with 1,000 employees can expect to spend $1.8 million a year to manage spam and lose $158,000 annually to virus attacks.[18]

Do you see any cause and effect to our vanishing balance? What are we to do when the 59 percent of us who use mobile devices are checking email in bed while in our pajamas, 53 percent while in the bathroom, 37 percent while driving, and 12 percent in church?

It is time to stop for a moment to think—and to do the math. Do we want email, or do we want balance? If we want both, we must adopt sensible boundaries. Consider an email quiet time, no email Fridays, checking only twice a day, not answering forwards, not hitting "reply all," keeping notes succinct, writing very specific subject lines, and not getting angry if people fail to reply. Personally, I'm not sure I will ever get to the bottom of my inbox—and that, too, is a survival strategy, to not obsess. If all else fails, follow the example of Stanford Law Professor Lawrence Lessig. Facing a seemingly endless inbox, he simply declared email bankruptcy.

Rx 11   Do the Math on Social Networking

A social-network service, according to Wikipedia, is about "building online communities of people who share interests and/or activities, or who are interested in exploring the interests and activities of others."[19] The recognition and use of social networking has been around for centuries, but the Internet has blasted it into the stratosphere. And the math is head-spinning.

Internet sites such as Facebook, MySpace, Twitter, and LinkedIn are familiar to many, but Wikipedia has an additional "partial" list of 155 sites[20] for our perusal. *"Please note the list is not exhaustive*, and is limited to *some* notable, well-known sites" (emphasis theirs). Social networking facilitates the radical democratization of connecting, networking, instant messaging, photo swapping, event sharing, job searching, promoting services, selling products, and so on. According to expert David Nour, it "is a mass collaboration platform accelerating one's ability to get things done."[21] Would I be revealing my age if I thought it's instead the *Titanic* of getting things done? As some want to celebrate the discovery of this New World, I want to hide under the table.

Use it with my blessing if it serves the higher priorities of life. But be cautious. Just be sure that after years of dancing in a circle you haven't used up all your mathematics yet not moved any further up the mountain.

Rx 12   Do the Math on Digital Pictures

Digital cameras have taken over. It is now possible to snap hundreds—no, thousands—of pictures at a single birthday party—*for free*. There are wonderful advantages to this new technology of course, particularly in emailing precious pictures to loved ones far away—*for free*. And you can afford to snap twenty quick pictures during the group shot, hoping you'll get one good one, and then just delete the duds—*for free*.

The problem is, someone forgot to do the math. "For free" is essentially a multiplication coefficient times infinity. Most people today have countless thousands of pictures on their hard drives, many of which they've never actually seen. When the pictures take up too much space, they're transferred to portable hard drives, jump drives, or CDs—where they remain unseen. I, for example, have 3,731 pictures on my personal computer in eighty-two files. And I don't even own a camera. When I retire, I look forward to going treasure hunting.

My wife, Linda, insists on using her old camera, the kind that actually has film. She sends more photos in more handwritten letters to more people around the world than anyone else you or I know. And she is loved for it.

Rx 13   Do the Math on Commutes

Having the option of living wherever we wish and commuting to work is a relatively new freedom, yet another benefit of progress. Nineteen percent of the total personal miles traveled in the United States involve this daily journey to and from work.[22]

The national average commute is 25.1 minutes each way per day, or 50.2 minutes roundtrip.[23] With 128 million people commuting, this translates into over *twelve millennia of time lost every day*. For each individual, the time spent commuting over his or her career will be the equivalent of two years of work time lost.[24]

I realize there are strong arguments to be made on both sides, most involving the higher wage earned from a distant job. But it is appropriate to calculate the opportunity cost. When a couple's average commute is one hundred minutes a day, something is gained in terms of money—but what is given up? I know of a couple that totaled four and a half hours commuting each day but had only three minutes of face-to-face communication. Do the math on that one . . .

Consider applying for some flex-time scheduling—perhaps an earlier or later start time when the traffic has thinned. Or working four ten-hour days per week. Or working from home one day per week. Some might wish to investigate moving closer to work or getting a job closer to home. A doctor from New Zealand read *Margin* and decided to buy a home closer to his office. And wouldn't you know it—God gave them the new baby they were so hoping for. Her name is Elizabeth.

Rx 14 Do the Math on Credit Cards

If we stacked up all the credit cards in the nation, the pile would reach seventy miles into space. The average household has five to ten credit cards depending on demographics. Each "payment due date" comes at a different time of the month, and with today's dreadful late-fee penalties, it is unthinkable to ever be tardy. The stress of hitting each payment date with unfailing precision one hundred times a year, for some families, exceeds the stress of the debt itself.

Of course it is wisest to eliminate credit cards altogether, but if the payment-due deadlines are punishing your psyche, at least cut down the number of cards to a bare minimum. Perhaps sign up for automatic payments through your bank. Or else send the payment back the same day you receive the bill. Yes, you might be early, but you will never be late. Our spirits need to be freed up for higher priorities.

Rx 15 Do the Math on Diet and Nutrition

The amount of food we take in must be balanced by the number of calories we burn off. The math is simple and inviolable. For example, a banana split at Denny's contains 894 calories. Jogging seventy-four minutes would burn this off nicely. Since most people I know do not have the inclination to jog seventy-four seconds, the math says we should pass on dessert.

At his eighty-fifth birthday party, a friend said, "If I'd known I was going to live this long, I'd have taken better care of myself." Exactly.

Rx 16 Do the Math on Sleep

In the days before the electric lightbulb, people routinely got nine and a half hours of sleep per night. There was not much else to do after sunset, and heading to bed was cheaper than burning oil and candles. But since 1900, the hours of sleep have consistently decreased. According to the National Sleep Foundation, we are now down to an average of 6.7 hours of sleep during workdays.[25] Not only did artificial light flood the night, but our modern lives have become complicated by longer working hours, shift work, caffeine, stress, anxiety, depression, telephones, television, video games, the Internet, and the NFL. When people are able to be active anywhere at anytime, often they are. As a result, our 24/7 cultural experiment has been accompanied by droopy eyelids. Seventy million of us qualify as sleep disordered.

Most people do best with seven to eight hours of sleep per night. Some need more—Einstein famously got ten to twelve hours per night and did not feel the need to apologize. Others need less. It is a matter of biology and mathematics. We each have a pretty good idea of our optimal sleep needs. And being adequately rested is a hallmark of a balanced life. So, shut off the computer, turn off the TV, switch out the light, and stop feeling guilty.

Everything we do, we do better well rested. The rested, stimulated brain thinks creative and productive thoughts. The exhausted brain thinks only of sleep. "Nature, to be commanded," said Francis Bacon, "must first be obeyed."

Rx 17 Do the Math on Stress

A friend and I were discussing the pressures of life, and I asked how his stress was doing. He has a national leadership role in a denomination and is required to make difficult decisions on a daily basis. He said there are two quantitative ways of handling stress. The first is when we keep stockpiling it in a warehouse. The warehouse fills over time and finally the roof explodes and the walls fall down.

The other strategy involves a train station. As the train moves down the tracks, the stress builds. But when it comes into the station, we unload our accumulated pressures onto the platform. Then we get back on the train as it pulls out of the station. I asked which illustration described him. He was a train-station guy. Personally, I'm a recovering warehouser.

/ / / /

If this seems to us a bit like an exercise in school mathematics, we wouldn't be far off. We always thought of school math as the dusty-book kind of thing where once we left the corridors of learning and entered the real world, we could safely forget about it. Quite the opposite. We have neglected our quantitative side for too long. If we are going to regain balance in a sustainable way, we need to know what is happening to our lives in understandable quantitative terms. It is important to realize that everything that costs us time, money, or energy must be considered and, when possible, recruited back onto the balance side of the ledger. Once we have plugged the leaks, we can begin to assign these resources to our higher priorities.

But this would not just be a mathematical victory, of course. This is a human victory, a relational victory, and a spiritual victory. We would live lighter, simpler lives with fewer decisions, complications, and stress. Our relationships, too, would be nourished with time, energy, and undivided attention. And our connections to God might once again be characterized by depth, prayer, and reflection. "Teach us to number our days aright," Moses wrote, "that we may gain a heart of wisdom."[26] Amen.

MAINTAINING A WORK-LIFE BALANCE

DWIGHT EVERHARDT'S LIFE revolves around farming. It is what he knows and what he does best. Like most farmers, Dwight is a hard worker. He and his wife, Bonnie, milk ninety cows from 4 to 6 a.m. and 4 to 6 p.m., 365 days a year. Rain, lightning, blizzard, influenza, broken bones—the cows must be milked.

Everhardt also raises cattle, a few horses, goats, chickens, grain crops, and 3,500 hogs on 2,500 acres in Pennsylvania. Last spring, during planting season, the forty-eight-year-old stoic felt strangely weary. "I had to hire another man to help me do chores," he said. "That's not me.

"I kept up my nonstop pace from sunup to midnight because that's the kind of person I am. The work had to get done," he said. "But then, all of a sudden, from the time I got up in the morning, the only thing I could think about was lying back down again."

One day during field work, Everhardt could not ignore the pressure in his sternum and some pain in his arms. A call to the clinic resulted in a treadmill stress test. He flunked it almost immediately. "It was kind of frightening how quickly the doctor made me stop."

When a subsequent angiogram revealed several blockages, he was helicoptered to a large specialty center in Pittsburgh. Balloon angioplasties were able to open the vessels, followed by stents to keep them patent. After an overnight in the hospital, he spent the next day resting at home. Then he returned to the barn.

Farming has never been an easy occupation, and with volatile dairy, grain, and meat prices, farmers like Everhardt are paying the price for today's chaotic work world. Out of necessity, love of the land, and inbred drivenness, they put in long hours "making the earth say beans instead of grass," as Thoreau put it. When we think of work-life balance, farmers have as much stress as anyone, but they also have an advantage—they live where they work.

The same can't be said for the jet jockeys. I fly a fair amount over weekends for conference speaking. By doing so, I log a lot of time with the Monday–Friday long-distance commuters. They often go out on a Sunday evening, stay at a residence-type motel, and then fly back home Friday evening. They might do this for up to a year at a time, and, let's just say, they often have issues.

Then there are the usual business travelers. When the plane lifts off, dozens of heads fall back and mouths flop open. Good night, and God bless America. Not all of them sleep, though. Some seethe. One Sunday I was landing at 11:00 p.m. The very moment the tires hit the tarmac, the guy next to me whipped out his cell, speed-dialed, and began screaming, "Well, heads are gonna roll tomorrow, and they're not going to be mine!" Given the chance, thirty or forty close neighbors would have tasered him. *It was 11:00 p.m. on a Sunday night.*

I met a pilot who flies the nonstop route from New York City to Tokyo. "Why are you headed to Minneapolis then?" I asked. "My family didn't like living in New York so we moved to Wisconsin." Oh. Of course. This means he jump-seats his way from Minneapolis to JFK, flies the fourteen-hour route to Tokyo, lays-over, flies the return route to JFK, jump-seats to MSP, and drives to western Wisconsin. Then he does it all over again. I asked when he sleeps. "Yeah, well," he said. "I'm always sleepy." A bit like those two pilots flying the Baltimore-Denver red-eye. Both were asleep on approach into Denver International, and their Airbus A319 was doing 608 mph instead of the required 287 mph. The tower's yelling finally woke them up.

Some LAX airline employees—about one hundred commuting pilots, mechanics, and flight attendants—camp out for $60 a month on Lot B, just down the road from Los Angeles International. The asphalt is broken and deafening jets fly continuously overhead, but the price is right. Many of the residents are separated from families for days or weeks at a time. "This is the cost of being a pilot today," said a first officer with Alaska Airlines. His wife and toddler son live in Fresno, a six-hour trip by car. "I've wanted to be a pilot all my life. It can be awful here. But I have to provide for my family, and I love flying airplanes," he says from his 1973 Coachman trailer. He is able to return to Fresno about eleven days a month but keeps in touch via webcam. "When my tires leave the driveway of my house in Fresno, the only thing I can think about is getting back to my family."[1]

The life of a doctor has also gotten tougher. One physician of the year told me every doctor he knew had burned out. "It's an occupational hazard," he said. A neurosurgeon confided, "I owe a million dollars, I'm operating night and day, and I've made three mistakes in the last three months." A second neurosurgeon opened a bagel store. Another doctor arrived home late after doing dictation—he finished his dinner prayer by saying "Richard Everett, MD." A medical student applying for our residency program fell asleep while I was interviewing him. I got him a pillow and turned out the lights.

But at least physicians have the advantage of living at home. Sort of. "I will never forget the death of a very well-known colleague," writes esteemed psychiatrist David F. Allen, MD.

He was deeply committed to his work. While making a night call to a patient at home he had a heart attack and died. A few weeks later his daughter consulted me. I was very sad because I loved her father; he was such a distinguished man. "I am so sorry to hear about your dad's death because he was such a great man," I said. And then she replied, "Dr. Allen, I know it is sad that my dad died. But the truth is I never knew my father as my daddy, I only knew him as 'the great doctor.' He was everybody's friend. He was good for all his patients, but he never had time for me. I never knew him. He is gone and I want to miss him, but I am missing the missing of him."[2]

Joe is a banker. As he rose up through the corporate ranks to become managing director of a major bank, he thought his workload would lighten. The opposite happened. "He now works six or seven days a week from multiple locations," reports the article "Extreme Jobs" from *Harvard Business Review.*

He keeps an apartment in New York, where he works two days, and is on the road another three or four days. Only on weekends does he see his wife and three children—who live in Connecticut. Even then, he gets calls in the middle of the night on Saturdays and Sundays, and flies out to see clients on a moment's notice. "The first year we were married," Joe's wife recalls, "we had to rearrange my grandmother's funeral so that he wouldn't miss a meeting."[3]

A U.S. congresswoman from a western state wanted to know the symptoms of stress and burnout. I rattled off fifteen or twenty. "What does it mean if you have all of those?" she asked. Then there's the burnout researcher from Columbia University who burned out. And the worker who yelled so loudly at his own boss that he ruptured a lung. Or the cable-news reporter who introduced himself on air but got his name wrong.

Explaining the Hemorrhage

Not only do we have increasing stress in the workplace, but it is simultaneously compounded by increasing tensions between work and home. That work can be stressful is not new. Nor is the reality that work can interfere with interests of broader life. But what is new—and yet another contemporary sign of the times—is the way these two issues have combined and then metastasized as never before. "I'd like to meet somebody who doesn't have problems with work-life balance," says Nancy

Costikyan, Director of the Office of Work/Life Resources at Harvard.[4]

The developments of modernity have led to a hemorrhage of time, energy, and attention *away from* family, community, faith, and leisure and *in the direction of* the workplace. This is not to suggest we have a conspiracy on our hands, but it is to point out that these powerful buffers of civilization have been compromised. As a result, work-life issues have become a prevalent topic in the fields of sociology, psychology, and family systems—as well as media outlets, coffee lounges, and high school reunions.

"The challenge of work-life balance is without question one of the most significant struggles faced by modern man. I've surveyed thousands of audiences about their greatest personal and professional challenges. Life balance is always at or near the top," writes Stephen Covey. "Despite all our gains in technology, product innovation and world markets, most people are not thriving in the organizations they work for. They are neither fulfilled nor excited. They are frustrated. They are not clear about where the organization is headed or what its highest priorities are."[5]

For job seekers and employers alike, work-life balance issues have now developed a permanent traction. Recruitment organizations recognize it as one of the most important workplace attributes, not only for purposes of recruitment but also for retention. Employees in sites more favorably inclined toward the issue report a higher overall job satisfaction. One company was so concerned about finding the proper work-life balance that it sponsored a conference to address the topic. To be sure everyone could attend and yet not miss work, the organizers scheduled it for Friday evening from 5:00 to 8:00 p.m. At least they tried . . .

All of this attention to work-life balance should be surprising considering the unanimous prediction of futurists half a century ago. Based on objective data and good science, trend watchers in the 1960s predicted that our problem today would *not* be overwork and work-life balance issues, but the opposite. They predicted an overabundance of leisure. In 1967, for example, testimony before a Senate subcommittee claimed that by 1985 people could be working just twenty-two hours a week or twenty-seven weeks a year.[6] No one scoffed. If this projection were extrapolated, today we would have one wage-earner per family working twenty hours a week.

When the muon was first discovered in 1937, Nobel Prize-winning particle physicist Isidor Isaac Rabi greeted its arrival with a surprised, "Who ordered that?" In much the same way, when the work-life balance phrase first fell out of the sky in 1986 and landed on our desks, it had people scratching their heads. On the face of it, it made no sense. We are smart, educated, articulate people with automation, technology, computers, and labor-saving devices—not to mention homes, automobiles, and a modicum of wealth. "Come on, people, we can figure this out. Why all the stress?" What are we so worked up about anyway? Where did all this come from, and why now?

Here's the real issue we should be pondering: If the pressures and stresses of work-life balance have intensified so unexpectedly over the past four or five decades, what will this look like in another twenty years?

A Catalogue of Changes

There are some who still don't believe things have changed. To them, work-life issues are just another sign that our nation has softened, our work ethic has eroded, and we've become a nation of touchy-feely complainers. Instead of seeing the widespread cultural resonance of work-life balance as an indication of escalating pressures all around, they believe it's a subjective issue best solved by an attitude correction.

Without, hopefully, sounding condescending, I've long noticed that most people are not trend perceptive. They see as far back as last week and as far forward as next week. Beyond that, the images blur. Life is full, and our days are crammed wall to wall. So perhaps this short horizon is understandable. Still, ignorance should not go uncorrected. It is critical that we understand the etiology of our disease. Only then can we prescribe an effective treatment and predict the future course of our ailment.

The following is but a partial list demonstrating how the workplace setting has changed, thus making work-life balance such a compelling imperative. We should review these trends in light of the larger narrative: the *more and more of everything faster and faster* of progress versus our relatively fixed human limits. We will not stop global progress (nor, in most cases, should we even contemplate it without careful consideration). But on a personal level, we can differentiate progress's hold on our individual lives more carefully. As we do, we will discover the ability to selectively move ourselves outside the equation as needed, setting our own independent personal and family course with balance in mind.

Global Economy—The global economy has grown dramatically and is now interconnected, integrated, and, at times, even tightly coupled. This leads to new opportunities but also new pressures, plus an unpredictable volatility. It also has expanded the international business cycle to a continuous twenty-four hours a day.

Technology—The nonstop arrival of new technologies necessitates continuous learning curves and adaptation. The average person today needs to learn how to operate over 20,000 pieces of technology a lifetime.

Complexity—The increase in the complexity of today's workplace is staggering to contemplate with the changes of technologies, computerization, procedures, rules, regulations, laws, services, products, markets, advertising, divisions of labor, modes of communication, as well as research and development integration.

Interruptions—We must deal with an unprecedented level of interruptions, as many as 200 per day. "Not long ago, information overload was the bane of office life—a deluge of data inundating our workstations and destroying our collective productivity . . . Now, though, there is a new workplace affliction: interruption overload," writes Rhymer Rigby. "People used to be able to interrupt you at work only by phoning or walking into your office. Now they can do so by e-mail, instant messaging, mobile phones (with voice calls and text messages) and BlackBerries or personal digital assistants."[7]

Work Hours—Instead of the predicted shortening of the work week, it has lengthened over the past fifty years. It now exceeds those of other industrialized nations. On top of this, many workers feel they are required to work beyond their capacities, especially if they wish to "get ahead."

Overtime—Employees are often asked to work overtime, beyond their scheduled hours. In many settings, putting in overtime is mandatory if a person wishes advancement.

Task Switching—The worker, according to an IBM document, starts doing something new every three minutes.[8]

Work Brought Home—The increase and the normalization of work brought home has been unchecked and often unchallenged. Technology gives us the ability to work anywhere, including at home, on the road, or on vacation—even in the bathroom. And since nearly 50 percent of office cubicle workers report their bathroom at home is larger than their cubicle, why not?[9] As a result, for many of us, work "is always on our mind."

Job Churn—According to the Treasury Department, "More than 55 million Americans, or four out of every ten workers, left their jobs in 2005. And this is good news, because there were over 57 million new hires that same year."[10] The process is called job churn, and it is usually regarded as a positive indication of job flexibility. Yet "churn" also serves as an apt verb for the economic and personal change this represents.

Job Insecurity—The foundation under today's worker is not secure. It makes little difference whether we worked locally for the Kmart store or Ford dealership, or if we were employed by Lehman Brothers, Enron, or Circuit City. The uncertainty concerning job futures often lies completely outside of the worker's control. Simply "working hard enough" is no longer sufficient to guarantee having a job.

Worker Loyalty—In an era of frequent job changes, there is less attachment to a workplace or institution. Loyalty is the feeling an employee has toward his company "when he has not had a better job offer within the previous ten minutes."

Commutes—For some, commuting is relaxing—a time to wake up at the beginning of the day and unwind at the end of the day. For most, it is a lengthening noxious experience. The longer commuting times, earlier commutes, later commutes, and more traffic intensity simply mean more time away from home.

Sleep Deprivation—The workforce has become drowsier than ever due to technologies invading the night (not only electric lighting but television and the Internet), in addition to earlier and longer commutes. One must also factor in the well-proven insomnia related to the increased stresses of modern living.

Changing Demographics—Our national characteristics continue to expand with mobility, immigration (legal and illegal), divorce, a later age of marriage, increasing numbers of singles, high numbers of single-parent households, an aging workforce, Baby Boomers working into their seventies, and the Millennials (Generation Y) entering the workforce. There are advantages but also challenges to this mosaic.

Changing Family Profile—The workplace is now populated with many different household patterns each with different needs. For example: (1) single without children, (2) single with children, (3) coupled-household with one wage-earner, and (4) coupled-household with dual wage-earners. Further complicating the picture is the age and number of children present in the household, from infants, to preschoolers, to elementary students, to teenagers. Each age represents its own unique challenges for a working family, particularly if no parenting figure is around for significant portions of the day.

Children—In 1900, 80 percent of American children had a working father and a stay-at-home mother; by 2000, it was 25 percent. Raising children and holding down a full-time job is a common scenario but, at a minimum, also a mathematical conundrum. An increasing number of young children are being raised by various configurations of childcare providers. By the millions, older children are more likely to come home to an empty house without guidance. Children's activities have also increased in scope—beyond homework and sports to language immersion and ballet. Most parents today have effectively lost control of the value structure of their children, and it frightens them.

Aging Parents—Baby Boomers, more than any previous generation, are required to deal with the time, money, health, and emotional needs of aging parents.

Speed—The increase in speed is evident both at work and elsewhere, and is often exhausting.

Stress—The rise in stress has been well-documented both inside the workplace and the family, as well as the broader society at large. In a survey by the American Psychological Association, one-third of Americans said they were living with extreme stress and 48 percent said it had increased in the previous year.[11] In the majority of studies, work and money are the greatest sources of stress. The economic burden of stress to industry is estimated at $300 billion annually. Seventy-five to 90 percent of visits to primary-care physicians have stress as a component of the symptoms. People bring the stress of their homes to the workplace, and they bring the stress of their work back to the homes.

Burnout—If the increase of stress is unchecked, it often leads to burnout and a high rate of comorbidity and related illnesses. This is commonly reported regardless the income level of the worker. A lucrative salary does not provide immunity from burnout.

Employer Drivenness—Some excessively driven employers demand impossible accomplishments with no excuses. One workplace motto says, "Perfection is expected; excellence will be tolerated." This can lead to a "high-stress, no exit" scenario, the most destructive of all stress circumstances.

The Female Factor—Women make up 47 percent of the workforce and 58 percent of college graduates. Organizations not offering flexible work arrangements experience a "female brain drain," especially during the years following the birth of a child.

Expectations—Both the employer and employee bring expectations to the workplace. Modern pressures and realities have shifted these expectations away from the traditional norms and, unfortunately, have sometimes widened the distance between the sides. If either side is unrealistic, it can lead to conflict.

Vacation—Workers who desperately need a break are not taking their allotted vacation time. It has also been reported that, recently, employees often use their vacation and leisure time for purposes other than rest and relaxation.

Boundaries—Boundaries between work and home are notoriously difficult to define and defend. The blurring often goes unchallenged and can be politically difficult for the worker.

Intensity—There is an increase in the intensity of work, which is related to the heightening of psychic vigilance and muscle tone. Increasing intensity will lead to mental and physical fatigue.

Violence—The rise of work-related violence is due to stress, interpersonal conflict, and general societal dysfunctions.

Absenteeism—There is an increase in the levels of asbsenteeism where workers commonly take sick days for personal issues unrelated to illness.

Workers' Compensation—There is a general increase in workers' compensation claims, especially for problems the workers would not have reported were they more emotionally invested in their work.

Recovering Balance to Work Life

To recover balance in our work life, we will first need to regain a sense of control. Nothing makes a worker or family feel more helpless, or more resentful, than when control is taken away and work concerns flood home every evening. This control, ideally, will not be characterized by an obnoxious pettiness but instead by equal parts responsibility, accountability, graciousness, hope, flexibility, and firmness. It helps to also throw in a touch of humor—if you can get them laughing, you can discuss just about anything.

The balance we need will not arrive passively on the overnight train from Toledo and be delivered to our door. It's something we need to work on, and the intentionality must be deliberate. What are our expectations? Are they reasonable? Is communication open and flowing? Do I have enough flexibility to adapt but enough firmness to keep the boundaries from crumbling?

As we choose prescriptions to match our needs, we'll remember that work and home are not inherent enemies but instead, God-ordained institutions designed to bless our lives.

Rx 1   Own the Problem

After presenting Grand Rounds in Internal Medicine at a large medical institution, it was time for the Q&A. The topic was work-life balance. The department chairman asked the first question: "What do we need to do here structurally to be sure that these doctors get more balance and margin in their lives? What kind of institutional changes?" This man is an insightful physician who is fully aware of his hard-working Type-A tendencies. On a personal basis, he doesn't really feel much stress from his long hours. But at the same time, because of his institutional responsibilities, he is well aware that every department surveyed had a red flag on work-life balance.

My answer: "You must own the problem." It is not easy for stoical physicians to admit limits or deficiencies. Our profession has always had broadly defined balance problems, but it's never been acceptable to discuss them openly. Yet if any of us is to make progress in work-life balance, we all must first admit that (1) humans have limits; (2) we are humans; (3) therefore, we too have limits; (4) the escalating process of progress will assault these limits; (5) exceeding our limits will not only harm our work and our life outside of work, but the balance between the two.

A healthy human, in both body and mind, requires sufficient exercise, adequate sleep, appropriate nutrition, meaningful work, nourished relationships, and spiritual connectedness. It is not a sign of weakness or immaturity to admit these needs. Nor is it suggestive of failure to say that we have limits. Actually, it's the first step in setting things right.

Rx 2   Decline with Gratitude

When asked to participate on a new project or committee, some say yes out of genuine interest. Others say it out of guilt, fear, or weakness. Five minutes later they run into the bathroom, stare at the mirror, and say, "What did I just do!" It's great to be a team player, and we should whenever possible. But in an era of proliferation from all directions, it's also important to read the fine print before signing on the dotted line. Balance is a fragile commodity, and it's best not to be dragged into a bottomless pit of obligation without our fully informed consent.

Dian Griesel is the founder and chief executive of a communications company in New York City. When asked by new clients about her willingness to travel for business, she quickly says no. "Sometimes they can't believe it. But because I've said it up front, it doesn't become a problem."[12] It's key to be polite and gracious but direct. Of course there are occasions when this does not go over well. But, then, it doesn't bother them if you miss your child's birthday.

Most people *over*estimate the repercussions of an appropriate "no," fearing wrongly that it might represent the end of a friendship or a job. They also *under*estimate the consequences of agreeing, as some commitments seem like small investments at first but can quickly grow.[13] Even when a reluctant obligation does indeed prove trivial, it can still leave us feeling resentful and "done to."

But if, against our better judgment, we accept a commitment, we might as well engage it with good cheer. Bitterness is a dark contagion. If we all drink from the same water, it makes no sense to poison the well.

Rx 3   Defend Boundaries

Most people cannot erect a fully opaque wall between their work and their home. Indeed, under most circumstances this would not be desirable. There will usually be a measure of mixing and crossing over. It's good to socialize, to be mutually supportive of co-workers' families during good times or difficult. It's appropriate, when possible, to go to office Christmas parties or company picnics and, perhaps if we wish, to participate in "take your child to work day."

But if a totally opaque wall is not what we are after, neither do we want a transparent one. A barrier that leaks continuously is little better than no barrier at all. In fact, it probably is better to have no barrier than a "pretend" one made of glass, a constant window where the workplace freely penetrates our home life.

More realistic is the idea of having a translucent boundary, a porous barrier, where some concerns bleed through—just not too much. This screen will allow for occasional work burdens to enter our home life. This simply means that we are human, that life is complicated, and that we care about our employer and co-workers. But the screen also has the capacity to filter out unwanted intrusions or excessive demands. In all this the family system needs to be comfortable and supportive about the crossings over, and not in conflict.

Many of the breakdowns in the work-life struggle come precisely at this interface. Boundaries between work and home have both blurred and weakened over the past three decades. A well-intentioned worker can become trapped in this demilitarized zone, caught between a demanding boss and an equally demanding family. Both sides need to be educated about how the principle works, and their compliance enlisted. It helps immensely if there is a sense of goodwill all around.

Lachlan Brown is president of a small business consulting firm specializing in Internet marketing. "I make it very clear at the beginning of any new business relationship that if I work nights and/or weekends then this is purely by choice. I've told clients more than once that if they call me at night or on the weekend that they shouldn't expect me to (a) answer the phone and (b) reply until the next business day." He has a nine-month-old daughter and refuses to see her grow up only in pictures.[14]

Once again, our long-term priorities help us clarify where to place the boundaries and how rigidly to defend them. Your co-workers won't be at your bedside when you pass, but your daughter might.

Rx 4   Have Several Gears

Many today have lost their transmissions. Speed is rewarded at the office, and, out of habit, we simply continue it twenty-four hours a day. "My house is on the median strip of a highway," says Steven Wright. "You don't really notice, except I have to leave the driveway doing sixty miles per hour."

I've always instructed the young residents that a good physician should have multiple gears, at least three: park, drive, fast. The middle gear, *drive*, is used for seeing the majority of patients. It's efficient enough to be productive and sustainable, but not so rushed we can't converse and, especially, smile at the babies.

Then there is the *fast* gear. It's used, for example, during flu season when we're triple-booked. Don't worry, I tell the young doctors—it's neither enjoyable nor sustainable, but we can do it. Always have. Just put on the track shoes and get through the day.

Finally, there is *park*. In many ways, this is the most important gear for medicine. And for life. This is the gear for telling the patient about the biopsy report. Or for comforting the person whose father just died in a car accident. Or maybe for giving the news that, after six years of trying, yes, the pregnancy test is now positive. In so many ways, these are the most important moments in the profession. It's unthinkable to miss them because our transmission got fried in medical school and we never had it replaced.

Carl Honoré is a London journalist and a recovering "speedaholic." "I love technology. I love speed. You need some things to be fast—ice hockey, squash, a fast Internet connection." But, he said, "My passion for speed had become an addiction. I was doing everything faster." His epiphany came while reading an appealing article about one-minute bedtime stories. He'd already cultivated the habit of speed-reading *The Cat in the Hat* to his son. "My first reaction was, yes, one-minute bedtime stories. My next thought was, whoa, has it really come to this?"[15]

Rx 5 *Obey the Speed Limit*

Every year the treadmill spins faster, yet another automatic consequence of progress. If we stay on the default cultural treadmill, the pace of our lives will accelerate continuously. It's gotten to the point where just about everyone I know has an earned PhD degree in speed. Have you heard about the whirlwind vacations? You can choose a one-night Caribbean vacation, a two-day African safari, or the three-night China tour.[16] How about the Minnesota state trooper who gave a ticket for 205 mph—to a motorcyclist? If we're driving 205 mph, it's hard to kiss the kids goodnight.

The world is drunk with speed, convinced that unless we fly faster than the speed of light, we will surely be overtaken. The motto of both work and home comes straight from Dickens: "The wind is rushing after us, and the clouds are flying after us, and the moon is plunging after us, and the whole wild night is in pursuit of us; but, so far we are pursued by nothing else."[17] We must keep running because, in Alexander Haig's priceless phrase, "we are subsumed in the vortex of criticality."

So velocity as a lifestyle is normalized because everyone in our frame of reference is speeding. The physicist says that on a jet we should be grateful for Einstein, because the peanut we're eating is moving 600 mph. If it weren't for relativity's frame of reference, it'd blow a hole through our head. A great theory, but we live on the ground.

Actually, *fast* is fine. I often enjoy going fast. At times it is appropriate and full of production.

Faster is also acceptable — usually.

But *too fast* — well, here we have a problem. Too fast is the same as hurry, and hurry is, by definition, dysfunctional. To break the speed limit of life is a breathless, gasping, wheezing, perspiring mistake. Any task performed while hurrying will need to be done over again. And again. "Ruthlessly eliminate hurry from your life," advises philosopher Dallas Willard.

Wisdom, worship, and love are slow, mellow, and deep. These will be in our room on that last day. But speed? It'll be twitching down the road, probably chasing tornadoes.

Rx 6 *Seek Periodic Technological Solitude*

The Finns have a tradition of seclusion. It happens in a small cottage called a Mökki, and there are half a million of them in a country of 5.2 million people. It's not like the country is pathologically reclusive; in fact, they are highly connected. Finland is the home of Nokia, the world's largest manufacturer of mobile phones. And it also has one of the world's highest rates of cell-phone ownership and Internet usage. But if the people are good at connecting, they are also good at disconnecting. If they are good at technology, they also are proficient at hiding.

Mökkis are relatively small and not particularly adorned. They can be in the middle of a city, such as Helsinki, but most are alone in a forest or near a lake. Finns love to retreat to these settings and look forward to not seeing another soul for days on end — perhaps weeks. The most striking feature of the Mökki experience is a serene, refreshing solitude.[18]

Back in the real world, technology has taken over. It's not as if we mind. Moderns have a love affair with technology in all its forms and regard it as one of progress's most marvelous gifts. But if we are entranced, we also are enmeshed. The downside of technology is real and painful, and it is the far-reaching tentacles of technology—directly or indirectly—that have caused the majority of our work-life problems. Now, do you want the scary version? We are still in the opening act. As pervasive as it is today, tech has only just begun its run. By the end of this century (assuming we make it that far), it is predicted we'll have a million times more technology than today.

It's time for the Finns to tutor the world. Occasional separation from anything pervasive is wise. But when dependence is this total, the ability to "fast" becomes almost mandatory. The question is, can we? By this I mean, are we capable? Can we build tech-free Mökki zones in the middle of our lives and use them for periodic disconnection and perhaps even occasional experiments in technological asceticism?

In the past, there was a closure on the end of every day, explain authors Charles and Janet Morris.[19] It was called night. There also existed a closure on the end of every week—it was called Sabbath, or the Lord's Day, or weekend. Technology, with our permission, has blasted that landscape clean. Today there are no natural closures, just as there is no natural solitude. How do we find our way back?

Perhaps by starting simply. It is possible, for example, to declare the first Thursday evening of the month—or *every* Thursday evening—as a technology-free Mökki zone. Or to check in to hotels in our own town to get away, as is already happening in record numbers. Perhaps we need to find a cabin to borrow, rent, or buy. Or take a three-day weekend pretending to live in 1850. Or a short disconnect for a reading evening or family meeting.

One Silicon Valley IT worker is a complete technological ascetic away from the job—no car, computer, or cell phone. The CEO of a Chicago public-relations firm forbids his employees from using their BlackBerrys after work or on weekends. He wants them to have family time, downtime, and rest. And he wants the same for himself as well. A physician complained incessantly about his busyness. I suggested he switch off his circuit breaker whenever he felt that way. That, apparently, wasn't the answer he was looking for.

Perhaps we need a silent retreat. Or a distant sabbatical, like the one I took on the Norwegian coast four hundred miles north of the Arctic Circle. Our family traveled on free miles and rented a hundred-year-old farmhouse near a fjord. It took us a month to get a phone connected. Or the six weeks I doctored in Carriacou, a tiny collection of mountains just north of Grenada. As part of my University of Wisconsin faculty responsibilities, we traveled to this beautiful but destitute and underserved island of 7,000 people. The entire population shared one gas pump. I was not phoned even once during that entire time—probably because there were no phones. No medical equipment either.

One rabbi suggests that the Sabbath is a day to stop our work, and it also is a day to stop *thinking* about our work. In Scriptures, the faithful not only disconnected for a Sabbath every week, but they also came apart for frequent biblical festivals. And then there were the prolonged desert visits. Dallas Willard maintains that Jesus was not at His weakest following forty days in the wilderness but rather at His strongest.

If we wish a healthy work-life balance, we will need to confront technology's hold on our lives. And, for some, such an examination might require a trip to the desert.

Rx 7 *Maximize Our Time at Work*

If we wish to have a life outside of work, it makes sense to complete our responsibilities expeditiously. If we dawdle it will mean, once again, another cold dinner. Here are some steps that will help (many of them not original with me): (1) Identify your prime time and pour most of your efforts into that space. Some are early birds while others are night owls. Plan work accordingly, if possible. (2) Control interruptions during sessions of productivity. (3) Batch tasks, such as email and voice mail. (4) Increase information selectivity. The sheer volume of information is beyond anyone's ability to assimilate. Therefore narrow the focus more precisely to those issues that matter most for the project. (5) Don't try to remember everything. Write down the important things and make an attempt to forget anything unimportant. (6) Prevent stress by becoming more organized, or prevent stress by letting yourself become less organized—and you know who you are. Both the hyper-organized and the sloppy worker waste unnecessary time and effort. (7) Nest your workspace. Set things up precisely according to your particular (and sometimes peculiar) needs. (8) Minimize body stress by making your work environment comfortable. (9) Prioritize your commitments for this work session. (10) If deadline motivated, schedule more time for a project near the due date and less near the beginning.

Rx 8   Maximize Our Energy

Time marches forward unchanging, but energy ebbs and flows throughout the day. Often we squander and misuse energy. We lack enthusiasm for our work, show up sleep-deprived and under-exercised, without a healthy breakfast, and spend our days listless, ineffective, bored, overloaded, or angry. At such times, our low energy leads to low accomplishment. We drag ourselves home, still limp, and hope that, somehow, maybe tomorrow will be different.

The thesis of Jim Loehr and Tony Schwartz's best-selling book *The Power of Full Engagement* is that energy, not time, is the fundamental currency of high performance. "Every one of our thoughts, emotions and behaviors has an energy consequence, for better or for worse. The ultimate measure of our lives is not how much time we spend on the planet, but rather how much energy we invest in the time that we have."

When we learn to skillfully manage our energy resources, it leads to a state of "full engagement" not only at work but in all the dimensions of life. "To be fully engaged, we must be physically energized, emotionally connected, mentally focused and spiritually aligned with a purpose beyond our immediate self-interest. Full engagement begins with feeling eager to get to work in the morning, equally happy to return home in the evening and capable of setting clear boundaries between the two."[20]

Rx 9   Get Adequate Sleep, Nutrition, and Exercise

Progress benefits us in many ways, but it also ushers in a host of pathologies. Because of progress (and our own culpability, of course) we are sleep deprived, overnourished, and deconditioned. As a result of electricity, we sleep two to three hours less per night than one hundred years ago. As a

uence, we purchase an abundance of food and consume it in
result of technology, we push-button our way through life and
thus seldom gain the conditioning we need—only 20 to 25 percent of us
have good levels of fitness.

One of the most effective ways to restore a feeling of balance at home
and work is through optimizing our physical health. Try eating nutritiously,
sleeping adequately, and exercising regularly for six weeks—in a serious,
rigorous way—and then assess the results. It is not easy to change habit
disorders. But a decreased consumption of television and food combined
with an increased consumption of exercise and sleep will work wonders.

Rx 10 *Beware Workaholism*

Any discussion of balance in the workplace must include a treatment of
Type-A behavior. On the one hand, no matter how cynical we wish to be,
these "extra-effort people" are owed a debt of gratitude. They have accomplished much, and the entire world has benefited from their enormous
work ethic. Believe me, if you have head trauma in the middle of the night,
you don't want me taking care of you. What you need is a workaholic neurosurgeon. On the other hand, if you don't recover well, it's best to let the
neurosurgeon go on to the next case—I'll take it from there.

Workaholism is called the respectable addiction. Many rewards follow.
The Type-A has character attributes that lead to success at work and rapid
promotion. These highly productive people often climb to the top of any
ladder by virtue of their dogged determination and fourteen-hour days.
But even as the drivenness pays off, it can disrupt both the home and work
setting. Not everyone can keep up, nor wants to. In the swirling cross-
currents, people get hurt. "My employer has adopted flextime," said one
woman. "I can work any eighty hours a week that I want."

Type-As don't know how to rest, suffer withdrawal when slowing
down, have inadequate warning signals concerning limits, and can be
impatient in relationships. Perhaps most importantly, they should beware
the quick temper. If unrestrained, the hostility often associated with
drivenness can lead to premature cardiac death.

A final note: Any lecture, article, or book on the topic of work-life balance written by a Type-A must be interpreted through that lens. In general, materials about work written *by* the driven . . . are written *for* the driven.

Rx 11 Investigate Flextime

There was a time—not that far back—when 8:00 to 5:00, Monday to Friday was standard for many jobs. But someone rolled a bomb in the middle of workplace uniformity, and by now it's been filleted into almost any configuration imaginable. Replacing its previous novelty status, flexibility has become a permanent fixture across the employment landscape. This is not to say that it is always accepted, especially by upper management. But the battle is essentially over, and work-life balance has won. The entrenched panzer divisions simply could not outlast the endless hordes of foot soldiers knocking on their doors and asking for concessions. First onto the beaches and scaling the cliffs were the mothers of young children who needed the work but also needed some time with little Ethan and Emma. How can anyone defeat the resolve of ten million mothers with workplace skills and homestead resolves?

It finally became clear that with 47 percent of the workforce being female (and nearly 60 percent of college graduates), this issue was not going away short of transgenderizing half the nation. As a result—with varying degrees of penetration—we now have such options as reduced hours, flexible workdays, job sharing, telecommuting, compressed workweeks, as well as off-ramping and on-ramping for the childbearing years. Some of the more traditional male workforce has joined the flex-timers, as have senior citizens. Businesses and institutions, too, have discovered this helps the bottom line due to savings in overhead and benefits.

Although this approach is not for everyone, the expanded menu of possibilities seems to benefit a significant percentage of the desperately work-life unbalanced. For those who do the research and ask the questions, sometimes the optimal job configuration can be found.

Rx 12 Be Productive with Margin

The Human Function Curve[21] (see chapter 5) illustrates the relationship between stress and productivity. Notice on this graph there are two times we are at 90 percent productivity: First, as the curve is sloping up; and second, as the curve is sloping down. In both cases we have the same productivity. In both situations we accomplish an equal amount. But the first time we hit 90 percent productivity—on the way up—we find ourselves working at a stress level that feels appropriate and sustainable. We have some margin in our lives, some space between our load and our limits.

In the second instance, however, yes, our productivity is 90 percent, but we have gone beyond the threshold of our stress limits. We have depleted our margin and are in overload territory. Fatigue is starting to build, and as we continue, it leads to exhaustion. Clearly, this cannot be sustained without associated dysfunction.

The implications are clear. If we wish to be highly productive in a sustainable way, we will try to stay to the left side of Point A—the infamous point of diminishing returns.

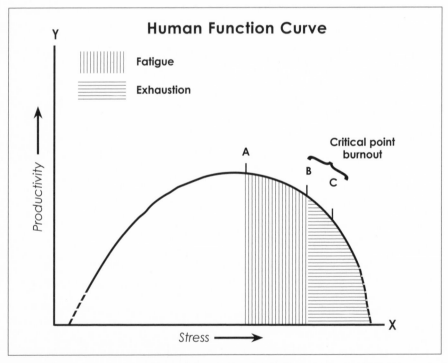

Stress Versus Productivity

Rx 13 Lower Expectations

The pursuit of work-life balance might require a lowering of expectations. This does not mean, of course, that we are settling for a mediocre life. Instead, it might simply indicate the changing of our compass. To jettison speed, clutter, consumerism, and long work hours in favor of a more reasonable pace and deeper relationships is not a loss.

But we must be realistic as there is often a price to be paid. One executive gave up the balance journey when he discovered "you can't have both a big paycheck and reasonable hours." I don't know why that surprised him. Perhaps we might need to accept a lower income if that is what's required. The question is, how much is enough? I can't answer that for anyone but myself. But I can point out that, first, expectations have steadily climbed over the past century to the point of an almost unreachable entitlement. And, second, our expectations are determined by the Joneses next door, not by any broader, historical, global, or eternal standard.

According to a recent Pew survey, time is the highest priority identified by people today. Sixty-eight percent of those surveyed said that "having enough free time to do the things you want" was a very important priority in their lives. In contrast, only 12 percent said that "being wealthy" was a very important priority.[22]

In his article "Rich Man, Poor Man," David Owen hit a diagnostic bull's-eye:

> You would think that simply not having bubonic plague would be enough to put most of us in a cheerful mood—but no, we want a hot tub, too. There is really no such thing as a rising or falling standard of living. As the centuries go by, people simply find different stuff to feel grumpy about. Every improvement in one's own situation is negated by an equal or greater improvement in someone else's. The easiest path to happiness would be time travel. If I took everything I own right now and moved it back 50 years, I would have it made.[23]

My discussion of expectation overload in *The Overload Syndrome* asserts that, of the sixteen types of overload discussed, this was the most difficult to conquer.[24] It often drives the entire train of trauma. Progress always heightens our expectations, and we willingly go along for the ride. But before we board that train, it's helpful to remember that "unrealistic expectations are but premeditated resentments." If we don't settle the issue of expectations versus contentment at the onset, it will mean problems later.

Just in case it's helpful to you, God has reasonable expectations of us.

Rx 14 *Delegate*

I was preparing to speak to the San Francisco leadership conference for a realtor's group when the president took me aside. "Everyone here has the power to delegate almost anything. If they have stress, it's self-inflicted." That was quite a statement, and, I suspect, an overgeneralization. Yet many people do have the authority to delegate but don't know how to use it. The more we can appropriately delegate away (not inappropriately "dump off"), the more time and energy we will have for both our work and personal lives.

This works not only in business but in the church as well. If others have spiritual gifts waiting to be used, it makes perfect sense to allow them that opportunity.

Rx 15 *Protect Time Off*

While in private practice, my day off was Wednesday. In order for it to be successful, I needed to leave town. We often did—and that was thirty years ago.

Today, it's not only physicians who have this problem. Sometimes dinner leftovers get thrown away, but work leftovers just pile up. Unfinished business sits on our chests and blows smoke in our faces. Literally millions of us are besieged by a perpetual to-do list in our heads. And that's not counting the phone calls, text messages, and bursting inboxes.

Our vacation time is less than most industrialized countries, and a large number of people do not even take the days available. For them, work is always "on." They've never been able to find the off button. People who use their time off to catch up on work are semi-happy to have decompressed that load, but they know it will grow back. Instead of feeling refreshed, their spirit is left chronically tired and resentful. Their learned helplessness follows them like a black cloud.

One entrepreneur started his first business at nineteen wh dent at MIT. He worked incredibly hard and was very successful first marriage failed, his girth swelled, and he was always exhausted. On a vacation with friends in Hawaii, he spent the first four days sleeping twenty hours a day. Finally his second wife said, "That's it." The wake-up call worked, and today he is an enthusiastic proponent of work-life balance. But sleeping twenty hours per day for four consecutive? Shouldn't that, in itself, be a red flag?

Small-business owners, the self-employed, and farmers know this problem inside and out. Of course it is challenging. But if they don't do the work, who will?

The pressures are real, and they are understandable. But these arrows are pointing in the wrong direction. People are healthier, happier, more productive, and more invested in their work if they can separate from it periodically. To push the delete button in our brains is essential if we expect to rest from our duties, recuperate from our stresses, and join family and friends for an occasional group hug.

Leave work at work. Take time off, and protect it. Guard personal time fervently. Resist the urge to check email. Turn off the phones during dinner. Get in the car and go somewhere. Shut out distractions. Don't schedule something for every moment of free time. Give full attention to the moment and to the people you are with.

Rx 16   Stay Off the High Wire

The high wire has its roots as far back as ancient Egypt. In first-century China, "rope dancing" was performed over knives.

In the 1850s, Jean Francois Gravelet received fame for cooking and eating an omelette—complete with stove and neatly set table—on a high wire stretched over Niagara Falls.

In 1945, Azerbaijan's sixteen-year-old Shafiga Bakhshaliyeva switched from studying opera to join the circus. Religious tradition forbade her from performing in public—let alone dressed in revealing costumes—so she moved to Moscow. Soon, she was dancing the fast-paced Lezginka on the wire. She continued for thirty years, touring Siberia when it was 61 degrees below zero and in Turkmenistan when it was 113 degrees above. "Some members of the audience even fainted from the heat. I was dripping with sweat, but the show had to go on."[25]

In the 1950s, Harold Davis, the Great Alzana, rode across the wire on a bicycle while carrying three women.

Karl Wallenda, blessed with almost supernatural balance, was the most famous. At age ten, he would sneak out of his apartment and perform in German *Bierstube* to supplement his family's meager circus income. Stacking chair upon chair, he would climb to the top and then push to a precarious but spectacular handstand, his feet nearly reaching the ceiling. Suddenly, he would shift his weight making it appear the entire stack was coming down. But he'd quickly recover, leap to the ground, bow, and collect his reward in coins and applause. In 1947, Wallenda created a routine no one has dared to copy, the seven-person chair pyramid. He walked the wire for over fifty years.

All that to say, stay off the high wire.

It requires astonishing balance, continuous practice, and perfect concentration. You must keep your eyes open, choose a single focal point, stay out of the wind, recognize early warning signs, be completely single-minded and almost insanely courageous. Plus you must understand physics—the center of mass, mass distribution, angular velocity, torque—your greatest friend at the most dangerous times.

If your balance is perfect, you know exactly what you are doing, and you know why you are doing it—then, perhaps, give it a try. But if you make a mistake, you're dead.

In the work world of high rollers, it is not uncommon for people to take great risks with foolish propositions. The resultant stress flows down the mountain as lava, engulfing family and co-workers alike. One spectacular flaming burnout is enough to char the landscape for miles around.

This applies not only to financial business risks but also to flirtatious behavior. Many people spend almost as much—or more—time around co-workers as around their families. In *The Bird in a Tree* (1940), author Elizabeth Goudge (one of our favorites) allows David's children to catch him in the midst of a moral compromise. It falls to Uncle Hilary, the parson, to chastise his nephew's dalliance.

God knows faithfulness to children is the most elementary principle of conduct under the sun, even the animals understand it. The
treatment of their children by many of the men and women of this
generation passes my comprehension. Your cruelty to them, for the
sake of your own selfish passions, is a thing I cannot understand.[26]

One foolish risk and it's possible to blow the entire castle off the face of
the earth.

A final note: Of the Flying Wallendas, Karl lost two sons-in-law to
chair pyramid accidents, and a sister-in-law and nephew to other falls. His
son, Mario, was paralyzed waist down. Karl himself fell to his death at age
seventy-three.

As I said, stay off the high wire.

Rx 17   Cherish the Home

I was speaking to a roomful of child psychologists and, at one point in the
presentation, was making an illustration about four-year-olds. I asked how
many in the audience had a four-year-old at home. A dozen hands shot into
the air. I pointed to the man closest to me and asked for his child's name.
Unfortunately, at that precise moment, he forgot.

I was as mortified as he was. We skipped the illustration, covered it
over, and romped quickly to the next point. It was one of those momen-
tary synaptic disconnects—I don't really hold it against him. But can you
imagine?

Then there was the busy family flying from Vancouver to Winnipeg
who arrived without their twenty-three-month-old son. Each person
thought the little guy was with some other family member.

My wife was eating lunch at a restaurant when a woman came in with
her young daughter, perhaps five. As soon as the waitress brought the
menus, the lady picked up her cell phone and talked for an hour. The little
girl ordered her food, ate it alone, then sat in silence.

How about the busy dual-executive family who hired a weekly taxi to
chauffer their daughter from school to her therapy sessions?

The family, traditionally, is the great shock absorber of society. But it has fallen on hard times. The shock absorber itself has been shocked. Sometimes it's the workplace that inflicts damage. Sometimes it's the ambient society. Sometimes, the wounds are self-inflicted.

If we wish to have a work-life balance—often called work-home balance—we first need a "life" and "home" to occupy that side of the equation. There are many things that can qualify as positive components, but for each of us, the family occupies a special position. Not everyone has a spouse and children to go home to at the end of the day, but we each have a family if broadly defined: parents, grandparents, brothers and sisters, grandchildren, nieces and nephews. Each is to be cherished. And each requires nurturing.

The book of Colossians speaks of such nurturing, saying we should clothe ourselves with compassion, kindness, humility, gentleness, patience, and forgiveness. And over all these, we are to put on love, which binds them together in perfect harmony.[27] What might the world be like if we all lived in such a place?

Shock absorbers and stability zones are possible, but they require time, energy, and work. "There are some basic forms of stability that every family needs," write Drs. Stevan and Ivonne Hobfoll in their book *Work Won't Love You Back*. "First and foremost, love must be stable. There must be no question but that those in the family are consistently loved and cherished."[28]

It has been stated that the greatest thing parents can do for their children is to love their spouse. If this relationship is anchored, the family's balance is greatly aided.

Love always wins. It's an undefeatable force. It is a type of currency, the currency of the relational life. When we spend love, the entire world becomes richer.

So let's hold our child's hand at the airport. Let's set down the cell phone at lunchtime. Let's drive our kids to the counselor's office and maybe even join the session. Then, at the end of the day, let's all go home together and put on love.

MEETING THE DECENT MINIMUMS

A NEW CATEGORY of hyper-intense professional was analyzed in the *Harvard Business Review* article "Extreme Jobs: The Dangerous Allure of the 70-Hour Workweek."[1] There have always been exceptionally hard-working people on every rung of the socioeconomic ladder, but this trend seemed to represent a new entity. The definition of "extreme jobs" not only required a minimum workweek of sixty hours but also other components of intensity, such as fast-paced work under tight deadlines, inordinate scope of responsibility, unpredictable flow of work, large amounts of travel, and 24/7 availability to clients.

Even though the stress was extraordinary, the remarkable feature of these road warriors was that they did not object. As a matter of fact, they loved their challenging jobs. By and large, instead of feeling exploited, they felt exalted. The severe hours put into their careers were matched only by the radical compensation they received as a result. They reveled in the work, the prestige, the responsibility, the opportunity, and the extravagant pay. They didn't really have a life outside of work, but neither did they seem to care. Life *was* work.

While the majority of those studied logged an average of 70 hours per week, many put in more. One man regarded a 90-hour workweek as his slow season, with 120 hours the norm. Even then, he often stayed later at the office despite having nothing additional to do. And he smiled talking about it.

For obvious reasons, the workplace became the center of their social lives. Home was often a source of stress and guilt, but, for many, work was the place of admiration and respect.[2]

These overachieving professionals would not even pretend to have balanced lives. Frankly, I don't think they cared. They'd chosen virtuoso excellence as their standard and were quite pleased with the results. Having achieved an unusual level of success in their career path, they were basking in the rarefied air of elite accomplishment. Basking, that is, if they ever had a free moment to bask.

Perhaps they are not aware that to achieve such a high level of ultra-excellence in one area of life automatically means they will suffer failure — or "negative excellence" — in other important areas.

Perhaps they don't understand about decent minimums.

The Nonnegotiable Decent Minimums

One psychiatrist, commenting on the "Extreme Jobs" article, observed, "It's not so much what these jobs require of us. It's the things they prevent us from doing." Life is made up of more than work, and every hour spent at work is an hour *not* spent doing something else. And what if the something *not* done had more intrinsic priority value than the work that displaced it? What if our business and busyness keep us from doing the things that matter most?

If our lives are wildly unbalanced by any single all-consuming activity — whether work, sports, television, or shopping, for example — it leaves us with a math problem. In the fixed environment of a twenty-four-hour day, we will have no time left for other important activities that require a decent minimum.

Often we divide life into two categories — work and everything else. While not an inappropriate way to analyze our personal world, I want to set that aside for a while. Let's instead look at two different categories —

the *optional* areas of life and the *non-optional* areas of life. What are those non-optional areas—the nonnegotiable and essential activities that we each must do (at least at some level) for our lives to be successful? And by "successful," I mean in the highest, noblest, most authentic sense of that word.

Described in other terms, what are the non-optional areas of life that require at least a decent minimum of our time, energy, and resources in order for us to avoid "negative excellence"? In other words, failure.

Take sleep, for example. We moderns have all manner of attitudes and behaviors regarding sleep. We resent it, claim it's a waste to time, play games with it, attempt to boycott it, try to cheat it, take pills to keep awake, and finally take pills to fall asleep. But whatever attitude we may have about sleep, and no matter how sternly we hold this attitude, sleep always wins. We must have a decent minimum of sleep. There really is no debate on this point. It is true for 100 percent of the earth's population. It is true whether we are a pauper or a billionaire, whether we work ten hours a week or one hundred hours a week, whether we have zero education or a PhD from Harvard. We all need sleep. If we do not sleep, we will have a miserable, dysfunctional life.

Let's switch from our human requirements for a moment and think about automobiles. In some ways, our lives and our automobiles have much in common. (I've often thought that physicians and auto mechanics did essentially the same job. They both take a history, do a physical exam, run some tests, prescribe a treatment, and if necessary perform surgery.) There is the optional side of car usage and the non-optional side. It's not enough to do only the optional parts of car maintenance, like washing and vacuuming. An immaculate car might be nice, but it is not essential. A car can go from Point A to Point B whether it's clean or dirty.

It's the non-optional aspects of automobiles that demand our attention—the things we dare not ignore. For example, we must put gasoline in the tank. We can't get very far on an empty tank. We also need to be sure the tires are inflated—we can't get very far on flat tires either. When we lift the hood, decent minimums stare back at us. We must have oil, antifreeze, transmission fluid, and brake fluid. The belts must be tight, and the hoses can't leak. The lights must work. And then there is the matter of obeying the speed limit, renewing our driver's license, buying auto insurance, and driving unimpaired.

If we want to succeed in using an automobile, we need to abide by the decent minimums. Each of these areas must be attended to if we wish to drive our car safely, legally, and for any length of time. This is not to say we need a $40,000 Lexus to accomplish our purposes. But we do need a vehicle with at least the decent minimum to complete the journey.

Humans are remarkably similar. There are many areas in our lives that require attention, at least at a decent minimum level. To be physically healthy, we need a basic level of exercise, sleep, and appropriate nutrition. We can't sit on the sofa, eat cream puffs, and watch movies for the next five years. Our emotions, too, need to be nurtured. Without a decent minimum investment, emotional health can be a fragile commodity. We need to work, not only because work is inherently good but because life requires money. We need adequate finances to pay our bills. Our family and friends need attention—we know that nourished relationships are an essential component of healthy living. Everyone requires a certain amount of leisure, a time to unwind, to recover from our efforts, to de-stress, and to experience diversion. We also need the spiritual component of life that connects us to the deeper things, the first things, the transcendent, the eternal.

Finally, I have one more category to add—and this one will surprise. We all need a decent minimum of imbalance. If we wish to be healthy, we will need some periods of disequilibrium, of growing, stretching, changing, and even suffering. Yet ironically, even our need for imbalance must be balanced. I promised earlier that we would discuss the proper role of imbalance later in the text and acknowledge its contribution to our well-being. We will honor that intention toward the end of this chapter.

As we consider these categories, several variables come to mind. For example, the amount of time, energy, money, and other resources we pour into each of these areas will vary from person to person, and also from week to week. In addition, some areas will get more resources than others.

But despite these variables, there is one universal: *Each area requires at least a decent minimum* investment of our resources to sustain health and well-being.

Graphing Our Lives

Here it is, then, laid out before us: Work—Finances—Family—Friends and Relatives—Physical Well-Being—Emotional Health—Spiritual Health—Leisure. To discover how this might help in our search for balance, let's make this list into a graph—a kind of life graph of our daily existence.

The next move is up to each individual, and it's an important one. How much of our "life" are we supposed to put into each area? By that I mean, how do we divide it up? How much time? How much physical and emotional energy? How much money, attention, and affection? These are complicated questions because it is often difficult to quantify such commodities. Instead, our tendency is to simply pour into each area what is required for that particular day. Perhaps the next day will be different. Perhaps not. We will find out tomorrow.

Most of us do not live with a high degree of day-to-day intentionality. To do so would probably be exhausting. Instead, we just let the day flow as determined by progress and the cultural norm. This approach is completely understandable—and it's also why we have balance problems.

Now let's go ahead and shape the graph. Somewhere out there reading this book, at this precise moment, is a forty-two-year-old married man with two children, a demanding fifty-hour-per-week job, and a one-hour daily commute. His name is Joe, and with his permission, we will graph his life.

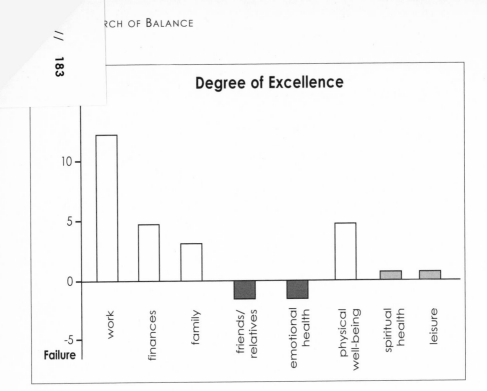

Looking at this graph,[3] we can make several observations. One is that Joe's degree of excellence in the work column is high. This is not a surprise since it occupies a significant part of his life. His finances appear to be good—evidently the job pays well and he doesn't overspend. But his spiritual health and leisure are both low. Of greatest concern, his friendships and emotional health are below the line, in negative territory. Anything falling below the line qualifies for what we might call "negative excellence." If he continues to violate the decent minimum requirement in these areas, he will eventually suffer the consequences—in this case, another friendless male with borderline depression.

He will most likely "feel" the imbalance and know that something is not quite right. But, because life is so full, he'll probably ignore the warnings and simply keep doing what is in front of him. And he will do it day after day after day. Joe would treat his car with more attentiveness than this. If the *CHECK ENGINE SOON* light comes on, or *OIL LOW*, or especially the *ENGINE OVERHEATED* indicator turns red, he would seek an immediate remedy.

Any area where the decent minimum is violated is an area that will experience dysfunction, often in pain and expense. This is not my idea. The statement flows directly from the definition.

The Uncomfortable Zero Sum

What can be done to correct these deficiencies? The graph has already served an important purpose in helping us visually illustrate the non-optional areas of our lives and, in the process, highlighting the areas of risk. The second step is the task of correcting these deficiencies. This simply means getting our lives back in balance.

We begin by facing an uncomfortable truth: We only have so much to spread around. Our resources are limited. We can't go out and buy more time, nor hire someone to love our families. If we need to exercise and sleep, we must do it for ourselves. I'm sorry to be so brutally clear in making this point, but life is, in many ways, a zero-sum game.

Recognizing this fact is the first step in setting things right. Admitting and accepting limits is a sign of maturity. Many of us never get this far. We keep entertaining the fiction that life is elastic, that we can stretch it like spandex. Of course, we can modify some of our resources—and we should learn to do that when appropriate. But using efficiencies, training, personal discipline, and even the appropriate use of technology will only carry us so far. Perhaps we might gain 20 percent more capacity than we have now. But then we will discover that we've simply relocated the threshold for zero-sum and must confront it all over again at the new level.

If we move our address into a higher capacity neighborhood, progress will simply find us there and re-create the same dilemma all over again. Progress is programmed to play its game of "more and more," while we play our game of "increase our capacities." But progress is *much* better at playing its game than we will ever be at playing ours. At some point, we need to change the rules of engagement and declare that we're not playing the "increasing more versus increasing capacity" game any longer. We're switching to the balance game.

The uncompromising truth is that whenever our lives are full, they are full. When progress jams us wall to wall with *more and more of everything faster and faster,* we become saturated. And once we are fully saturated, life is a mostly closed system. Oh, we can continue to pile things into our lives, but the effect will be to further overload the system and compound our imbalances.

This is not as dire as it might sound. Not at all. We still have many avenues to explore, and there are options available to us. But once we have accepted the truth of the zero-sum closed system, going forward is easier than it seems. For many of us, half our stress melts away once we realize it's better to be supersane than Superman or Superwoman.

A verse in Philippians says, "I can do everything through him who gives me strength."[4] This is a favorite verse for many, and I love it as well. It is completely true, reliable, and a great comfort. But it doesn't mean what some have taken it to mean. When Paul said, "I can do everything" (other translations read, "I can do all things"), he did not mean we can walk across the Atlantic Ocean or swim across the Pacific. We can't go a year without eating. We can't ignore sleep and stay healthy, out-shop our income and remain solvent, or work twenty hours a day and still love our families. Everything God has given us to do, He will also give us the strength to do it. In all things we are to be dependent on His power rather than our own. Then He will give us the power to do His will. And in this process, as we shall soon see, a great many advantages begin to flow through the spiritual resources God makes available to us.

Restoring Balance by Protecting the Decent Minimums

Within a closed system such as our graph represents, we can move some resources from one column to those that lack. This is the first option to consider. Any column too high might be coaxed into sharing resources with an area in need. We can be more intentional, rigorous, and creative in doing this than we typically settle for. One less meeting at work, for example, can mean more time with the children. One less hour of leisure in front of the television might mean an extra hour walking with a friend.

There is a significant possibility, however, that the process of sharing between columns might not yield enough resources to balance all areas. Thankfully, we still have options to consider. One immediate benefit comes by discovering that our "closed system" is not, after all, completely closed. This is hopeful news. Still, no matter which direction we turn, choices need to be made. The trouble, Martin Luther said, is that we try to change while keeping ourselves intact.[5] We will never achieve the balance we need unless something in our life changes.

Rx 1   Use the Efficiencies of Combination

Because life is an integrated whole, everything is connected to everything else. Life in that sense is like a mobile—we pull one part and the entire mobile dances. Sometimes this means that one dysfunctional part can sabotage our entire existence. But it can also work the other way around. Investigate the possibilities of combined positive action in two or three areas at the same time. Take exercise, for example. If we do exercise walking with other people, we can accomplish three things in one act: fitness, stress reduction, and building friendships. Gardening, for those who enjoy it, can help simultaneously in multiple areas: emotional health, finances, and physical well-being through exercise and good nutrition. Carpooling is yet another. If the logistics are feasible, it can save money while simultaneously building relationships.

Rx 2   Establish a Decent Maximum

In addition to the concept of a decent *minimum*, there are some areas where we should establish a decent *maximum*. If balance is our goal, we must not allow any area to become too greedy. For example, if the work column is allowed to rise too high, it will—all by itself—preclude balance from being possible. A second example—if a person is exercising for two hours a day, he or she is doing so for reasons other than fitness. In the process, exercising is robbing resources from the other columns. In the area of finances, perhaps we have a good bank account flush with money. But if we are shopping twenty hours a week, this is stealing from other areas.

Even if we *can afford* this in financial terms, we *cannot afford* it in terms of our time, energy, attention, and affection. Our quest for life balance has other uses for these resources.

Rx 3   Take from the Trivial and Routine

Our graph only represents the non-optional areas of life, yet our days are also occupied by hundreds of things that do not fit into these categories. We might call them optional, routine, or trivial—but whatever we call them, we have them in abundance. Perhaps we can spare a few for our more pressing needs.

In a hotel parking lot one morning, we saw a man waxing, and waxing, and waxing his truck. The only times he would pause from his vigorous efforts were to glare at his children and yell at them, repeatedly, to get back inside the hotel. What a strange scene. How disproportionate. Buffing a truck for hours while yelling at children. Almost enough to break the heart of the asphalt.

I shouldn't pick on this fellow—he had his reasons. Probably a tough morning, or a tough marriage, or a tough job. Actually, perhaps we should thank him for holding up a mirror. How we live and what we love—after a while, it begins to add up.

So in memory of our truck buffer, perhaps we might walk around our lives with a flashlight and collect all our optional, routine, and trivial activities. Next, we will put them in a box. Finally, we'll sort through them and see if we can convince any to share. Surely we can extract a few minutes from manicuring the yard with a toothbrush, over-the-top collecting, doting on pets, looking through catalogues, stockpiling magazines, watching soap operas, buying lottery tickets, playing Internet poker, routine over-cleaning, compulsive social networking, playing computer solitaire, surfing the Internet, video gaming, contributing to hyper-proliferated kids' sports, shopping for fashion, buying too many shoes, going off-list in the grocery or hardware store, eating out, recreational and addictive shopping, watching too much football, camping out in front of *American Idol* reruns, over-planning birthday parties, running for daily cappuccinos, and eating candy. And, of course, that is just a beginning . . .

One physician acquaintance has a 1930s' classic car collection as a hobby. "I sold my favorite antique because of you," he told me. I grimaced at the insinuation that my advice had brought him unhappiness. "Oh, no," he assured me with a smile. "You don't know how good it feels to be finished with that debt."

Rx 4   Displace Your Television

If we own a television and watch it with some frequency, we cannot *possibly* tell God, ourselves, or our families that we have no modifiable options available for achieving balance.

Rx 5   Follow the Counsel of Your Heart

In the residency where I taught, to be clinically competent upon graduation was the cherished final product for the young doctors. In the process of discovering how a physician attains such a goal, we discussed the long hours of study, consulting the right academic sources, gaining experience through direct patient care, attending medical lectures, and learning from peers and attending doctors. Yet there was one more aspect of competence that I would frequently emphasize—clinical instinct. I can't completely describe how we come by this valued commodity, but once a doctor has it, he or she learns to trust and follow it. You not only "think" and "see" and "hear," but you also "feel" what is wrong with the patient. I learned to trust my instincts, I would say, almost more than any other input.

One elderly doctor was the sole physician in a small town twenty miles from our hospitals. His style was, at times, almost laughably antiquated. Yet his patients would drive one hundred miles and wait hours to be seen by him. Frequently he would send patients for admission to our internal-medicine service. The residents would call the faculty and complain about yet another "dump," an inappropriate admission for vague symptoms. Their initial screen indicated this person should never have been admitted. I would smile. "Well, let's just give it a day or two and see what turns up." More often than not, our geriatric clinician had sharp instincts, and the patient had significant illness.

One pulmonologist, in addition to being a very pleasant individual to work with, had the best clinical instincts I have ever seen. When I'd consult in the middle of the night from the Intensive Care Unit, he would invariably tell me exactly what the patient needed—even if still in Stage 1 sleep. He was always correct. It was uncanny.

We, too, are in a training program on life balance. Not necessarily by reading this book, but simply by living in this culture. We are all swimming in the same maelstrom, trying to figure it out. Life-balance issues are difficult. There are many prioritizing decisions to be made in the process of regaining equilibrium and stability. So we research, study, discuss, and ponder all the information. In the end, our instincts—centered in our own heart and spirit—will often be the best guide.

This all presupposes, of course, that our intentions are pure, our conscience is clear, our integrity is high, and our character is trustworthy. It requires, too, that we are quiet enough, wise enough, and humble enough. If we bark loudly to intimidate the universe, it will thunder back at us, unimpressed. God does not ask my counsel, and I do not offer it. But He has placed within us a spiritual gyroscope, the Spirit of God.

If we try to understand how a gyroscope works, we will come away still scratching our heads—angular momentum, axle, torque, gimbal, precession, pitch, roll, yaw? But as a balancing device, the gyroscope is mysteriously spectacular—keeping jets, the space station, and even the Hubble oriented in the sky. We too have a mysterious, even miraculous guide that transcends books and science. Learn what the promptings of the Spirit feel like, and take care not to grieve His heart. "Whether you turn to the right or to the left, your ears will hear a voice behind you saying, 'This is the way; walk in it.'"[6]

Rx 6   Guard Family Decent Minimum

The family is far too important—and too fragile—to live on a diet of leftovers. Yet the way our society and work environments are currently structured, we often give the least time to those we value most. When a family is strong, nothing can compare as a God-ordained vehicle of love, affirmation, and stability. But this takes work. It takes time, goodwill, and communication. Today's family also takes prayer—lots of it. And it certainly requires a decent minimum.

The family requires a decent minimum for communication. We often are so busy we don't communicate clearly. It takes time and energy to listen carefully. An office worker wrote himself a computer reminder: *Talk to wife*. One man stopped for gas in Ohio and was ninety miles down the road into Pennsylvania before he realized he'd left his wife back at the station. In contrast, when we were first married, Linda says she'd come up from the basement with the laundry, and I'd tell her how much I missed her. (I'd also hold her hand while she was frying bacon.) We are not quite that breathless anymore, but just to be sure the Ohio-Pennsylvania syndrome never strikes, she drives me to the airport and picks me up when I return. This might sound like a waste, since it would be easy for me to drive myself. But efficiency is the furthest thing from our minds. This routine gives us eighty minutes each way to talk about my trip. It's been quite an unexpected blessing.

A marriage takes a decent minimum for intimacy as well. Art Linkletter asked a little boy what his mom and dad did for fun. "I don't know," the kid said. "They always lock the door." Today we don't need to lock the door—we're too exhausted to get caught in any interesting positions.

After intimacy come children, and they need a decent minimum as well. "Time is not your friend; it's your enemy," said Haddon Robinson, speaking to physicians about children and busy lives. "If you don't spend time with them when they are six, you'll never get six back again."[7] I watched a recent fascinating movie titled *Children of Men*. (As a policy, I don't recommend films, and this was difficult to watch in many regards.) The dystopian story takes place in England in 2027, eighteen years after the world had inexplicably lost its fertility. In a world without children, every scene reflected the absence of hope. The landscapes were filthy, anarchy was everywhere, the violence nonstop. At one point, an ex-midwife says, "As the sound of the playgrounds faded, the despair set in. Very odd what happens in a world without children's voices."[8]

Jesus, too, loved hearing the children, and once it even triggered His anger. The Creator, Sustainer, and Redeemer of the universe was fuming. His disciples were only trying to help—protecting Him, guarding Him from the crowds, triaging access. But when Jesus saw them rebuking those bringing the children to their Shepherd simply for a touch, "he was indignant. He said to them, 'Let the little children come to me, and do not hinder them, for the kingdom of God belongs to such as these.'"[9] If this set Him off, it gives me pause to think He's watching us now . . .

Place priority on family and build a strong sense of family. Have family meetings and reading evenings. Spend time with your children; hang around together; have one-on-one times. Demonstrate unconditional love. Have bedtime rituals. Show physical affection at all ages. Laugh together and spread goodwill throughout the family. Grant grace; teach and model reconciliation and service. Say thank you twenty times a day, and keep the family's mind on the pleasant aspects of life. Consciously slow the pace of life. Establish stability zones. Guard the dinner hour. Experience shared faith. Pray together.

Rx 7   *Guard Imbalance Decent Minimum*

Balance is not only valuable but also essential for peaceful, well-adjusted, enjoyable living. But even if perfect balance were attainable, it would be unwise to remain in that state continuously. Every week, every month, every year we will invite imbalance to penetrate our lives for specific purposes. Strategic imbalance is the place of appropriate change—growth, challenge, development, experimentation, training, exertion, discipline, learning, stretching, and increased demand. And, yes, even suffering.

A move to a different city, for example, is imbalancing. Sometimes it is a welcome change, and we feel excited about the different house with all its possibilities. It is invigorating to get a new start in a different neighborhood and to meet new people. But moving can also be dreadfully stressful. Would we want to do that every three weeks?

To change jobs, buy a different car, have a baby, or even get a different style haircut—all can be energizing. And perhaps each change listed is movement in a positive direction, something that will bring improvement and add a new sense of freshness to our lives. But each is also destabilizing in the sense that each disrupts the norm.

The first month of having a new baby in the house—as glorious as that event is—can be disruptive for everyone. But as soon as possible, we move to "normalize" the disruption by adapting the home to the baby's needs and demands. After establishing a schedule and factoring in new expectations, the house can resume a measure of equilibrium and restedness.

To seek additional education—whether community college, tech school, the university, or post-graduate—can be a significant challenge. Anyone who has studied for a difficult make-or-break test knows the pressure this setting brings. Still, afterward, we are richer, fuller human beings with expanded horizons. But do we want to study for a killer test every week of our life?

Even our bodies' fanatically protective homeostasis has accommodation for change built in. Imbalancing forces are welcomed into our physiology on a continuous basis, as long as the process of homeostasis can do its superintending work of harnessing the new change into the overarching structure of order and stability. To train for a marathon, lose fifty pounds, or recover from an illness—each represents a "stressor" on the body, but in a good way. Homeostasis knows how to monitor and guide these developments to guarantee they proceed in a healthy, moderate fashion.

Frustration often arises when imbalance is thrust upon us by others without our permission. If our lives are disrupted in this way without any decision control on our part, energy and attention are consumed by irritation. And these resources are then lost for the purposes of our higher priorities.

A life that never experiences *balance* is a life of constant instability and disruption. A life that never experiences *imbalance* is one without growth and challenge. To be healthy, we require a good "balance" of both.

Rx 8   Befriend Simplicity and Contentment

It is hard to imagine regaining balance without the help of our timeless friends, simplicity and contentment. Given the need of the era, it almost seems they have risen to the status of patriarchal axioms. With the world becoming inexorably more stressful, overloaded, complex, intense, and cluttered, to say nothing of faster (all mathematical statements), it seems incomprehensible to manage such challenges without making routine pilgrimages to these fundamental biblical concepts. Every column on our life graph can gain strength from these two giants.

I gave a presentation at the national meeting of a medical-specialty society a decade ago. Afterward, there was a small circle of questioners engaging the topic for another twenty minutes. All the time I could see a woman from the corner of my eye, standing to my right, along the wall by a curtain, listening to our discussion but pretending otherwise. She obviously had something to say but did not feel comfortable saying it before her peers. Finally, the last of them melted away and I turned in her direction. "Thank you for your talk," she said softly. "I crashed and burned six years ago. Since then, I've tried continuously to simplify my life. After six years of intensive effort, I've finally gotten it down to 100 percent."

People often ignorantly believe that simplicity and contentment are effortless—just plop down in a chair, close your eyes, sigh deeply, and quit trying. But as this physician demonstrates, it is a mistake to think them an easy acquisition. Overload is actually the easy one. To achieve overload isn't difficult in the least. Just stay on the default treadmill and overload will come to us without the slightest effort on our part.

On the other hand, simplicity and contentment are difficult disciplines to court. But once ingrained into our lives, they bring a sense of freedom that is truly bountiful.

In some ways, this is a struggle format. First of all, we struggle with the power of our culture. The prevailing doctrines of comfort and affluence must be conquered. We swim against the crowd, the sentiments of the media, and every personal insecurity we've ever battled.

Spiritually, too, these disciplines are strenuously acquired. Simplicity and contentment both involve a countercultural restraint. They require hanging a public *Not for Sale* sign on our affections, no matter the price. We're always digging deeper—not for gold but for the timeless priorities. We allow things to pass by because we are on a much larger, much higher journey than that. We walk the mountain path and must travel lightly. We follow a different leader down a different road for a different purpose to a different destination.

We do this, not because it is easy, but because it works—we need this blessing on our lives. And we do it, especially, because it is true. In this sense, simplicity and contentment are the example of Jesus. They are way of the Gospel, the way of the cross, the way of freedom. If it is hard, it is also right. If it is a difficult task, it is also richly rewarding. There is no feeling that compares to living the truth of Jesus in an authentic way.

"To be a worldly person is, in fact, to be a 'practical' or 'functional' atheist," writes Tullian Tchividjian in *Unfashionable*.

> It's someone who — despite all he professes — lives and makes daily decisions as if God doesn't exist. A practical atheist is a person who comes to conclusions about money, business, worship, entertainment, ministry, education or whatever else without the directing influence of God and his revealed truth (the Bible). Instead, for him, cultural assumptions and societal trends serve as the directing influences for how he thinks, feels, and lives . . . *Christians make a difference in this world by being different from this world; they don't make a difference by being the same.*[10]

Simplicity and contentment are two cousins, clearly of the same lineage but varying in their mandate. Simplicity is merely commended in Scripture. Contentment, however, is both commended and commanded. Paul *commends* contentment in his letter to the Philippians: "I have learned the secret of being content," and in his first letter to Timothy: "Godliness with contentment is great gain." And in Hebrews, it is *commanded*: "Be content with what you have."[11]

To me, simplicity and contentment are the two sides of the Great Doors into the cathedral of practical biblical freedom. Christ taught both, endorsed both, exemplified both. There is no higher endorsement.

Some feel this is a pauper's life, but they are missing the point entirely. The deepest riches come only to those who pay the price. The treasure that abides is one that cannot be bought or even owned. It is given us freely by God. We must certify it with our own consent.

When Wendell Berry said, "We must achieve the character and acquire the skill to live much poorer than we do,"[12] he was not speaking about suffering deprivation but about escaping entrapment. The writer of Hebrews told us to "throw off everything that hinders."[13] Augustine once said that God is always trying to give good things to us, but our hands are too full to receive them.

If we do not understand this today, it will become clearer as we near the Jordan. Everything, as a matter of fact, will become clearer along that final journey. And simpler.

Dr. David Allen writes,

> Some years ago I worked with a very distinguished professor of medicine who was dying of cancer. Her word to me was this: In spite of the pathos and the pain, dying is very simple. There is no need for long talks or conversation or complex relationships or meetings. Unexpectedly, after being very ill, the professor was healed of the cancer and returned to health. She told me then that she wished she could live in health like she had lived when she was dying. "David," she said, "Remember that life at its heart is very simple. When we are facing death only the basic things are necessary. Once we move out of illness we complicate our lifestyle and live beyond our means and make life more difficult for ourselves."[14]

Rx 9   Use the Multipliers of Faith

God is not surprised by our dilemma with limits and decent minimums. It is precisely the way He set it up. We have limits. He created those limits. It is OK with Him that we have such limits. He is not limited by our limitations. He does His best work in the face of our limits. He makes His power available to us. If we truly wish to effect change in ourselves, in those around us, and in the world, it will be through God's power and not our own.

As a result, our best resource—by far—in dealing with the constraints of our relatively fixed limits is in direct appeal to God. From the tiniest particle of our lives to the massive unsolvables—He is near, waiting an invitation to work on our behalf.

In emotional health, for example, God has said, "Do not worry about tomorrow."[15] He also said, "Do not be anxious about anything; do not be afraid; and do not fret."[16] That's already helpful. Then He created music to calm our troubled moods. We know music is therapeutic, but we just don't know why, nor does science know where it comes from. He gave us four-year-old children to laugh every four minutes. Laughter, too, is highly therapeutic for reasons not well understood—except by God. He gave us nature to lift our spirits with a mountain, a deer, a stream, a bluebird, a prairie, and a sunset. If we had to pay rent for looking at a flower, imagine the cost.

He gave us the gift of prayer and is surprised when we don't use it. Someone has said, "A life without prayer is a boast against God." Martin Luther wrote, "Pray, and let God worry." This is good theology. We have not because we ask not.

In our relational well-being—whether family, relatives, or friends— God endorses it all enthusiastically. "Two are better than one," He says.[17] He gave us to each other for purposes of benefit. To demonstrate how that works, He asks that we care for one another. We are to serve one another, carry one another's burdens, and pray for one another. In the process, all are built up. When we love others, we are simultaneously loving God—and ourselves.

In our work and finances, God is there. He prods us a bit, saying we must work if we wish to eat. But He also loves a cheerful and diligent worker. Our ability to labor is a wondrous blessing. As Rudyard Kipling said, "The glory of the garden glorifieth everyone."[18] God also insists we receive a fair wage so we have enough to live on and to pay at least our decent minimums. He speaks of living a life of restraint so we might avoid worrisome debt, and then have the joy of helping others, for "it is more blessed to give than to receive."[19] Everything we need, He has already provided.

In physical well-being, God expects us to care for ourselves. He made the human body more marvelous than anything on earth or the known universe. We are fearfully and wonderfully made, crowned with glory and honor, and we bear His image. We are to care for our body, for we are not our own—we were bought at a price.

You see, when we attend to our spiritual health, we attend to every aspect of our well-being. There are over 1,500 studies that examine the relationship between faith and health, and almost all find a positive association. This grants us access to a huge multiplier. When we exercise, we love God at the same time. We love God whenever we love our spouse, children, or friends, when we serve our community, when we sing, plant flowers, go for a walk, or feed the birds. God gives hope at every turn, and hope is health enhancing.

We did not create the air we are breathing right now. Nor did we instruct our lungs to inhale. We didn't create the food we eat, nor the ground in which it was grown, nor the ability of the seed to germinate. We didn't instruct our GI tract to digest. We didn't tell our brain to acquire language. We didn't tell our initial single cell to grow us. We did not create the 10^{28} atoms in our body, nor did we instruct a trillion trillion of them to turn over in the next hour, all in balance.

It is grace. "From the fullness of his grace we have all received one blessing after another."[20]

Love is the greatest multiplier. Whatever it touches, it heals. And when it is used, it always increases.

CONCLUSION

10

SECURING A SPACE FOR DEEP CONSECUTIVE THOUGHTS

WE LIVE OUR entire lives in *this present moment*. It is impossible to live next week in next week. It's only when next week becomes *this present moment* that we live it.

How narrow, do you suppose, is this present moment? Five seconds? One second? 1/1000th of a second?

There is a teaching in the Talmud that this present moment is infinitely narrow. When we stop to ponder, of course, it must be true. This present moment is, literally, so narrow that it is impossible to conceive. We live our entire lives in an inconceivably thin slice of reality.

Reflecting on this for many years now, I have arrived at a corollary understanding—that *this present moment* is not only infinitely narrow but also infinitely deep. I have no proof for this conviction other than the essential nature of both God and infinity.

Sometimes I lie in bed, lights off, eyes closed, Linda already drifted down, and I try to slow time. I try to slow my thoughts, my breathing, my muscles, my heart—everything. I try to slow the moonbeams coming in through the window. I try to stop the nitrogen atoms from hitting my tympanic membrane. Just lie there without motion and without sensory awareness. I'm trying to peel away every aspect of reality that consumes my attention until only one thing is left: time. I'm trying to *feel* time so I can enter into it. Instead of living above time as we do — skimming rapidly along on the surface of life — I want to enter its flow.

My purpose is to somehow gain access to *this present moment*. There is a sense in which I am trying to crawl up to the event horizon of this present moment and peer over the edge into infinity. I've attempted this now a thousand times.

I wonder if I can somehow slowly approach the edge and look down, if I will be able to see our little Nico. Please forgive the silly contemplations of a grandfather, but when Nico died last year, at eleven months, he left us many gifts. One was depth. He *wants* us, even from beyond the grave, to know that he waits for us. Where time stops and infinity begins, that is where we will find him waiting.

Nico's second birthday would have been this past July, so we gathered at Adam and Maureen's for the remembrance celebration. After cake, stories, laughter, and tears, they asked if we would watch Katja for a while so they could run an errand. When they returned, Adam rolled the inside of his left forearm to show us his tattoo.

Abyssus

Abyssum

Invocat

07-07-07

It is Latin for the majestic phrase "Deep calls unto deep" found in Psalm 42:7.

"Deep calls to deep in the roar of your waterfalls; all your waves and breakers have swept over me." The psalmist was in the midst of great affliction: his soul downcast, his bones suffering, his tears for food. Yet his soul, even in its sorrow, yearned for God. He saw the waters plunging down Mt. Hermon roaring into the swirling depths, and there he met the presence and power of God. "Why are you downcast, O my soul? Why so disturbed within me? Put your hope in God, for I will yet praise him, my Savior and my God."[1]

Following this phrase was Nico's birthday, 07-07-07. He was born on the perfect day—the seventh day of the seventh month of the seventh year, and it was on the seventh day of the week, a Saturday.

Adam thought about it for a year and then, finally, made the decision. He scheduled it on Nico's birthday. He wanted his deep wound to be visible, and, at the same time, to give lasting testimony to his abiding love for his perfect little boy. He hopes people ask him about it.

We have our Nico to remind us of the things that matter most. He has added both weight and depth to our hearts. But what of the world? I fear for any society that has lost its depth.

Riding the Light

Einstein once commented, "If you want your children to be brilliant, read them fairy tales. If you want them to be geniuses, read them more fairy tales." When he was sixteen, he had a "fairy tale" thought experiment about riding a beam of light. This insight of his early genius held implications that were not solved until ten years later.

After graduating from Zurich, Einstein sent out résumés across Europe but could not gain employment. *You act like you're smarter than we are* was the general response. Finally, he landed a part-time job as a patent clerk in Bern, Switzerland—the very definition of under-employment. In May of 1905, he visited his good friend Michele Besso, who also worked at the patent office, and discussed with him the problem that had plagued Einstein for a decade—regarding light, either Newtonian mechanics was right or James Clerk Maxwell's equations were right, but they could not both be right.

Eventually, totally exhausted, Einstein announced that he was defeated and would give up the entire quest. It was no use; he had failed. Although Einstein was depressed, his thoughts were still churning in his mind when he returned home that night. In particular, he remembered riding in a streetcar in Bern and looking back at the famous clock tower that dominated the city. He then imagined what would happen if his streetcar raced away from the clock tower at the speed of light. He quickly realized that the clock would appear stopped, since light could not catch up to the streetcar, but his own clock in the streetcar would beat normally. Then it suddenly hit him, the key to the entire problem. Einstein recalled, "A storm broke loose in my mind." The answer was simple and elegant: time can beat at different rates throughout the universe, depending on how fast you moved . . . He had finally tapped into "God's thoughts." He would recall excitedly, "The solution came to me suddenly."

The day after this revelation, Einstein went back to Besso's home and, without even saying hello, he blurted out, "Thank you, I've completely solved the problem."[2]

Without depth, we have no fairy tales. And without fairy tales, we have no riding on beams of light. And without riding on beams of light, we have no streetcars racing away from clock towers. And without streetcars racing away from clock towers, we have no Einstein. Without depth, we have no Einstein. In exactly the same way as, without suffering, we have no Dickens.

The Right to Think

Few things frustrate me as the absence of deep consecutive thoughts. I crave the dimension of depth. When life becomes too busy, I storm around the house ranting, "I *need* deep consecutive thoughts."

What will happen to a generation that has lost its concept of depth? Life has devolved into an endless sequence of twitching. How will we ever penetrate *this present moment* if we don't stop twitching? At the end of our lives we will discover that hurry was only a socially glorified form of perspiration.

Modernity is very good at a great many things, but not a single one connects to depth. Einstein once said, "It's not that I'm so sma.. that I stay with problems longer." Yet we have no longitudinal attention span today. Instead, we have "continuous partial attention." Technology has enhanced our productivity and simultaneously destroyed our depth.

"Technology has sped everything up and, by speeding everything, it's slowed everything down, paradoxically," said John Challenger, CEO of a Chicago-based outplacement consultant group. "We never concentrate on one task anymore. You take a little chip out of it, and then you're on to the next thing. It's harder to feel like you're accomplishing something."[3]

What does it mean when the average worker, according to IBM, starts something new every three minutes?[4]

Depth is born out of such disciplines as stillness, patience, solitude, waiting, intimacy, suffering, quiet, contemplation, submission, discipline, prayer, and yes, margin and balance. Modernity, on the other hand, is suffused with such "non-disciplines" as speed, interruptions, noise, multitasking, clutter, alarms, advertisements, distractions, Twitter, texting, television, viruses, entertainment, cell phones, activity obesity, information overload, and the Internet.

Physicist and professor Michio Kaku (who gave us the Einstein story) maintains that our most advanced computer today has the intelligence of a cockroach. (The infrastructure of our economy is now being maintained by a swarm of cockroaches?) Our computers only know the difference between zero and one. That's all the higher they can count. They do it very rapidly and very faithfully; they can handle exabytes of information in impressive fashion. But they have no wisdom. They have absolutely no depth.

Seneca was a Roman philospher who lived at the time of Christ. In his famous essay "The Shortness of Life," he said, "Everybody agrees that no one pursuit can be successfully followed by a man who is busied with many things . . . since the mind, when its interests are divided, takes in nothing very deeply."[5]

Chuck Swindoll, after a twenty-five-year ministry in the Los Angeles area, transitioned to the presidency of Dallas Theological Seminary. During this time of change, he had one clergy confide, "Nobody around me knows this but I'm operating on fumes. I am lonely, hollow, shallow, enslaved to a schedule that never lets up." For Swindoll, this triggered a wider survey of the landscape filled with pressures and exhaustion.

> One of the growing concerns I have entertained as a result of this temporary time of appraisal is the busyness of so many in the [church]. Pastor and parishioners alike have often confided in me, admitting that the "tyranny of the urgent" is not a theoretical issue, but a very real fact of life. It leaves them feeling strung out, impatient, occasionally resentful, and even worse, empty . . .
>
> For almost twenty-five years my family and I lived in the Los Angeles area . . . I must confess that I found myself becoming weary of the noise, the crowds, the pace, the relentless press of activities, the never-ending rush of traffic. While we thoroughly enjoyed the people, the opportunities for ministry, and certainly the weather of that area of the country, there were times we ached for relief . . . for the essential presence of stillness, of silence.

Dr. Swindoll's diagnosis is compelling: "An absence of intimacy with the Almighty. Involvements, yes, but not intimacy. Activities and programs aplenty but not intimacy."[6] He suggests a return to simplicity, silence, solitude, and surrender.

Tom Peters, the best-selling business author of all time, wrote a piece for *Forbes ASAP* titled "Please, I just need some quiet time." He recently built a new house on Martha's Vineyard that is only accessible by rowboat. Then you transfer your load to a jeep with deflated tires. The house has no electricity and no phones. "We are isolated by design," he says.

At 5:15 a.m., he is rowing across the glassy bay.

> I have—can you believe it?—thoughts. I want to see. To be fresh. I want to matter. To do that I need to be at Cape Poge. Or I need to be on my farm [in Vermont] . . . The right to be left alone is—the right to think . . . How I need to be a-w-a-y. To have s-p-a-c-e. To reflect. The world—call it convergence—is closing in on

us. All of us. And I believe that my/our number-one requirement is—SPACE.[7]

Would I?

Balance is directly related to my concerns here. An imbalanced life implies stress, disharmony, and agitation. A balanced life seeks serenity, calmness, and moderation.

Speed belongs to the former, depth to the latter.

If all our motion is horizontal and our pace is best characterized as rushed, how will we ever penetrate the infinite depths of this present moment? Our hasty superficiality might yield productivity in one sense, but it will never be profound. And it will never find God.

Ravi Zacharias commented on the thirst for speed and experience among today's university student.

In an article for *The Chronicle of Higher Education* [University of Virginia English professor Mark Edmundson] attempts to describe the turbo-charged orientation of his students to life around them. "They want to study, travel, make friends, make more friends, read everything (superfast), take in all the movies, listen to every hot band, keep up with everyone they've ever known . . . They live to multiply possibilities. They're enemies of closure . . . [They] want to take eight classes a term, major promiscuously, have a semester abroad at three different colleges, [and] connect with every likely person who has a page on Facebook."

Edmundson argues that for all the virtues of a generation that lives the possibilities of life so fully, there are detriments to the mind that perpetually seeks more and other options. For many, the moment of maximum pleasure is no longer "the moment of closure, where you sealed the deal," but rather, "the moment when the choices had been multiplied to the highest sum . . . the moment of maximum promise."[8]

"What does it profit a man," asked Christian Danish philosopher Søren Kierkegaard, "if he goes further and further and it must be said of him: he never stops going further; when it must also be said of him: there was nothing that made him pause?"[9]

If the angel Gabriel came during the night, would that make us pause? Perhaps to tell us we were the recipient of a great honor, chosen by God for an epic task. The details were not revealed, only that we must remain continuously ready. The event would come in a month, or a year, or a decade, but the timing was not our concern. God would attend to that. Our sole assignment was to be ready.

To be continuously ready . . . a daunting thought. Always watching, always waiting, always alert, never drifting. Required, absolutely, to stay on task. Living within a single focus: just One thing.

We wake, yet even in the darkness we know the angel was real, that we have been summoned. I wonder: Would we want this assignment? Would we accept this privilege with its almost impossible requirements for focus? Do we know how to access deep sanctified spaces when called upon to do so? It distresses me to consider how ill-prepared I am for such a challenge.

My favorite poem is "The Wise" by William Everson.[10] It is an accounting of the Magi who gave their entire lives looking for a sign. They spent decades watching, years in pursuit, month after interminable month reading the wrong texts. Their days were consumed with charting, their nights knotted in thought.

Then it appeared. The mark had been made.

They dropped everything, leapt on their camels, and headed furiously in the direction of the Sign. Gone were the wasted hours, the drabness, the frustrations, the repeated despair of empty hope. All was left behind, swallowed up in the glorious knowledge that the preparation was now over and culmination lay just over the horizon.

In the center of the poem is this triumphant line: "For when the mark was made they saw it."

Would I?

NOTES

CHAPTER 1—DREAMING THE POSSIBLE IMPOSSIBLE DREAM

1. Keith H. Hammonds, "Balance Is Bunk!" *Fast Company*, December 19, 2007, http://www.fastcompany.com/magazine/87/balance-1.html.
2. Marshall Goldsmith, *Harvard Management Update* 13, no. 11, November 2008.
3. Dana E. King, MD, MS, et al., "Adherence to Healthy Lifestyle Habits in USD Adults, 1988-2006," *The American Journal of Medicine* 122, no. 6 (June 2009): 528–534, http://www.amjmed.com/article/S002-9343(08)01207-2/fulltext. From 1988 to 2006, the percentage of those with overweight body mass increased from 28% to 36%, those achieving physical activity twelve times per month decreased from 53% to 43%, those eating five or more fruits and vegetables per day decreased from 42% to 26%, and those with moderate alcohol use increased from 40% to 51%.
4. Sandra Tsing Loh, "Let's Call the Whole Thing Off," *The Atlantic*, July/August 2009, 116–126.

CHAPTER 2—HOW AGGRESSIVE PROGRESS SABOTAGES THE BALANCE WE NEED

1. 1 Chronicles 12:32.
2. *Macbeth*, act 5, scene 5, 19–28. Shakespeare wrote in the 1500s, but

his play *Macbeth* took place in the eleventh century. In 1040, the main character—patterned loosely after the Scot Mac Bethad mac Findláich, known in English as Macbeth—captured the throne by killing the ruling king, Duncan I.

3. Beatrice and Ira Freeman, "About Bagels," *New York Times*, May 22, 1960.

4. Matthew 13:24-30,36-43.

CHAPTER 3—HOW BALANCE IS DISPLAYED IN EVERY QUADRANT OF THE CREATED ORDER

1. Moe Norman materials were drawn from a dozen sources, the four most helpful being: Bruce Selcraig, "Golf's Purest Striker Rarely Missed a Fairway," *USA Today*, September 9, 2004, 9C; Guy Yocom, interviewer, "My Shot: Moe Norman," *Golf Digest*, November 2004, http://www.golfdigest.com/magazine/myshot_gd0411; Brent Kelley, "'Unknown Legend' Moe Norman Dies," September 5, 2004, http:// golf.about.com/b/2004/09/05/unknown-legend-moe-norman-dies .htm; "The Feeling of Greatness: The Moe Norman Story," http://www .moenorman.com/.

2. John Milton, MD, PhD, Professor of Computational Neuroscience, Claremont College, "The Brain and Brawn of Athletic Performance," January 12, 2005, http://faculty.jsd.claremont.edu/jmilton/reprints/ chicago_05.pdf.

3. Richard A. Swenson, MD, *More Than Meets the Eye: Fascinating Glimpses of God's Power and Design* (Colorado Springs, CO: NavPress, 2001). These and other facts about the human body are contained in part 1.

4. Sherwin B. Nuland, MD, *How We Live* (New York: Vintage Books—Random House, 1997), 30, 33.

5. Nuland, xviii.

6. Apostolos P. Georgopoulos, MD, PhD, "Movement, Balance, and Coordination," *The Dana Guide*, November 2007, http://www.dana .org/news/brainhealth/detail.aspx?id=10070.

7. Randy J. Guliuzza, MD, "Beauty in Motion," *Acts & Facts*, May 2009, 10–11.

8. Nuland, 41.

9. K. C. Cole, quoting Sir James Jeans, *The Universe and the Teacup: The Mathematics of Truth and Beauty* (San Diego: Harcourt, 1997), 10. Sir James Jeans said: "The Great Architect of the Universe now begins to appear as a pure mathematician. The universe can be best pictured, though still very imperfectly and inadequately, as consisting of pure thought, the thought of what we must describe as a mathematical thinker."

10. Peter D. Ward and Donald Brownlee, *Rare Earth: Why Complex Life Is Uncommon in the Universe* (New York: Copernicus of Springer-Verlag, 2000), 266.

11. Fred Heeren, *Show Me God* (Wheeling, IL: Day Star Publications, 1998), 197.

12. Also assisting Jupiter and Saturn are Uranus (14 times Earth's mass) and Neptune (17 times Earth's mass). In contrast, Mercury is 0.05x, Venus is 0.8x, and Mars is 0.1x.

13. Ward and Brownlee, 240, 51, 37.

14. Ward and Brownlee, 37, 265.

15. Paul Davies, *Cosmic Jackpot: Why Our Universe Is Just Right for Life* (Boston: Houghton Mifflin, 2007), 149.

16. Davies, 146.

17. Davies, 85.

18. William Craig Lane, "Cosmos and Creator," *Origins & Design* 17:2, http://www.arn.org/docs/odesign/od172/cosmos172.htm.

19. Lane.

CHAPTER 4—HOW TO PLACE YOUR LIFE IN STABLE ORBIT AROUND YOUR PRIORITIES

1. Steve Jobs, "Stanford University Commencement Address," June 12, 2005.

2. Pluto's perihelion (closest to the sun) is 2,755, 800,000 miles, and its aphelion (farthest from the sun) is 4,538,700,000 miles.

3. Bureau of Labor Statistics news release, June 2008, examined the number of jobs that people born in the years 1957 to 1964 held from

age eighteen to age forty-two. The title of the report is "Number of Jobs Held, Labor Market Activity, and Earnings Growth Among the Youngest Baby Boomers: Results from a Longitudinal Survey," www .bls.gov/news.release/pdf/nlsoy.pdf.

4. "How to Begin a Biblical Ministry to Job Seekers in Your Local Church," A Career Transition Ministries Network White Paper, June 6, 2008, 3, http://www.ctmnetwork.org/downloads/CTM-White%20Paper.pdf.

5. "I, the LORD, do not change" (Malachi 3:6). "Keep your lives free from the love of money and be content with what you have, because God has said, 'Never will I leave you; never will I forsake you'" (Hebrews 13:5).

CHAPTER 5—HOW TO COUPLE BALANCE (*EQUILIBRIUM*) WITH MARGIN (*CAPACITY*)

1. National Transportation Safety Board (NTSB) report of the Aaliyah crash, http://www.ntsb.gov/ntsb/brief2.asp?ev_id=20010907X01905& ntsbno=MIA01RA225&akey=1.

2. "Aaliyah Plane Was Overloaded by Hundreds of Pounds," cnn.com/ World, August 31, 2001, http://archives.cnn.com/2001/WORLD/ americas/08/30/aaliyah.crash.

3. NTSB report of the Keith Green crash, http://www.ntsb.gov/ntsb/brief .asp?ev_id=20020917X03242&key=1.

4. Gordon Gibb, "Plane Crashes: A Primer for Keeping It Together in the Sky," April 28, 2008, http://www.lawyersandsettlements.com/ features/plane-crash-keeping-it-together.html#.

5. Richard A. Swenson, MD, *Margin: Restoring Emotional, Physical, Financial, and Time Reserves to Overloaded Lives* (Colorado Springs, CO: NavPress, 2004), Figure 5.1, 55.

6. Marty Nemko, "Smart Ways to Give Your Career a Boost—Simple (and savvy) tips from a career coach, no charge," *U.S. News and World Report*, May 2009, 27.

7. Marcus Yoars, "Too Busy for God," *MinistryToday*, August 3, 2007, http://www.ministrytodaymag.com/blog/2007/08/too-busy-for-god .html.

8. "The LORD is my shepherd; I shall not want. He maketh me to lie down in green pastures: he leadeth me beside the still waters. He restoreth my soul" (Psalm 23:1-3, KJV).

CHAPTER 6—COUNTERING THE ESCALATION OF THE NORM

1. Sally Ann Lasson, "Warren Buffett: The Secret of the Billionaire's Success," February 16, 2009, http://www.independent.co.uk/news/ business/analysis-and-features/warren-buffet-the-secret-of-the -billionaires-success-1622649.html.

2. CNBC, interview with Warren Buffett, November 20, 2006.

3. Marvin Olasky, "Personal and Political," *World*, April 14, 2007, 40. (The phrase "'*Nekulturny*' the Russians would say, not cultured activities for a leader" is most likely Olasky's who has lived in Russia and speaks the language.)

4. Economist Herbert Stein (1916–1999) was a senior fellow at the American Enterprise Institute, on the board of contributors of *The Wall Street Journal*, chairman of the Council of Economic Advisers under President Nixon and President Ford, and professor of economics at the University of Virginia. He developed Herbert Stein's Law in the 1980s. He also is the father of Ben Stein.

5. "The Nation's Long-Term Fiscal Outlook," August 2007 Update, United States Government Accountability Office (GAO-07-1261R).

6. Because of the effects of the recession, this 2008 figure of $292,600 was already $21,000 lower than the average 2007 cost of $313,600. The square footage was higher in 2008 than 2007 however.

7. http://most-expensive.net/wedding-bouquet.

8. "Cremation Statistics," http://www.uscremationequipment.com/ index.php?option=com_content&view=article&id= 54:cremation-statistics&catid=42:cremation-statistics&Itemid=68.

9. Max Alexander, "The Surprising Satisfactions of a Home Funeral," *Smithsonian*, March 2009, http://www.smithsonianmag.com/ arts-culture/Presence-of-Mind-Which-Way-Out.html.

10. Rachel S. Cox, "A Movement to Bring Grief Back Home," *The Washington Post*, June 5, 2005, A01, http://www.washingtonpost.com/

wp-dyn/content/article/2005/06/04/AR2005060401667_pf.html.

11. Elinore Pruitt Stewart, *Letters of a Woman Homesteader* (Boston: Houghton Mifflin, 1913 and 1988), 190–191.

12. "Take my yoke upon you and learn from me, for I am gentle and humble in heart, and you will find rest for your souls" (Matthew 11:29).

13. "Let your gentleness be evident to all" (Philippians 4:5).

14. "Man looks at the outward appearance, but the Lord looks at the heart" (1 Samuel 16:7).

15. Erik Richardson, "The Economics of Time," in *Get Satisfied: How Twenty People Like You Found the Satisfaction of Enough*, ed. Carol Holst (Westport, CT: Easton Studio Press, 2007), 140.

16. Dennis Overbye, "Physics Awaits New Options as Standard Model Idles," July 4, 2006, http://www.nytimes.com/2006/07/04/science/04phys.html?_r=1&th=&pref=slogin&emc=th&pagewanted.

17. "God, the blessed and only Ruler, the King of kings and Lord of lords, who alone is immortal and who lives in unapproachable light, whom no one has seen or can see" (1 Timothy 6:15-16).

18. "God is light" (1 John 1:5). "God is love" (1 John 4:16).

19. "Rich wounds, yet visible above" is from the hymn "Crown Him with Many Crowns," by Matthew Bridges in 1851. The third stanza: "Crown him the Lord of love, Behold his hands and side, Rich wounds, yet visible above, In beauty glorified. No angel in the sky, Can fully bear that sight, But downward bends his burning eye, At mysteries so bright."

20. "You are my friends if you do what I command. I no longer call you servants, because a servant does not know his master's business. Instead, I have called you friends, for everything that I learned from my Father I have made known to you" (John 15:14-15).

CHAPTER 7—DOING THE MATH

1. Rick Moranis, "My Days Are Numbered," Op-Ed contributor, *The New York Times*, November 22, 2006, http://www.nytimes.com/2006/11/22/opinion/22moranis.html.

2. Vitaliy Ankov, "Probe into Claim Jets Sold for $5 Each in Russia's

Volga Region," *RIA Novosti*, June 8, 2009.

3. *Telegraph* Obituaries, John Bachar, July 23, 2009, http://www
.telegraph.co.uk/news/obituaries/sport-obituaries/5895468/
John-Bachar.html.

4. Obituary: John Bachar, *The Economist*, July 18, 2009, 84.

5. Attributed to Richard Lamm, former governor of Colorado.

6. We are speaking here in terms of our practical experience of time and
not the physics of relativity. Relativity teaches us that time is elastic
relative to velocity and gravity.

7. "But the fruit of the Spirit is love, joy, peace, patience, kindness,
goodness, faithfulness, gentleness and self-control" (Galatians
5:22-23).

8. Pat Katz, PAUSE—The Voice of Sanity in a Speed Crazed World, vol.
8, no. 35, November 12, 2008, http://www.patkatz.com/.

9. Shamsi T. Iqbal and Eric Horvitz, "Conversations Amidst Computing:
A Study of Interruptions and Recovery of Task Activity," *Proceedings
of the Eleventh Conference on User Modeling* (UM 2005), June 2007,
Corfu, Greece, http://research.microsoft.com/en-us/um/people/
horvitz/conversational_interruptions.pdf.

10. Tom McGrath, "Do You Have Office A.D.D.?" *Men's Health*, October
2007, 173.

11. Nielsen wire, "Americans Watching More TV Than Ever; Web
and Mobile Video Up Too," May 20, 2009, http://blog.nielsen.com/
nielsenwire/nielsen-news/americans-watching-more-tv-than-ever.

12. Taylor Gandossy, "TV Viewing at All-Time High, Nielsen Says," CNN,
February 24, 2009, http://www.cnn.com/2009/SHOWBIZ/TV/02/24/
us.video.nielsen.

13. Norman Herr, PhD, Professor of Science Education, California State
University, Northridge, "Television and Health," 2007, http://www
.csun.edu/science/health/docs/tv&health.html.

14. University of Michigan Health System, "Television (TV) and
Children: Your Child," updated July 2009, http://www.med.umich
.edu/yourchild/topics/tv.htm.

15. "Ideas from IBM—You've got (too much) mail," October 20, 2008,

2, http://www.ibm.com/ibm/ideasfromibm/us/email/20081020/
IFI_10202008.pdf.

16. "E-mail Spam," Wikipedia, http://en.wikipedia.org/wiki/
E-mail_spam.

17. Ideas from IBM, 1.

18. Sara Radicati, PhD, editor, "Email Statistics Report, 2009–2013,"
The Radicati Group, Inc., http://www.radicati.com/wp/wp-content/
uploads/2009/05/email-stats-report-exec-summary.pdf.

19. "Social Network Service," http://en.wikipedia.org/wiki/
Social_network_service.

20. "List of Social Networking Websites," http://en.wikipedia.org/wiki/
List_of_social_networking_websites.

21. "The Future of Social Networking," Herman Trend Alert, July 29,
2009.

22. Marcus Bowman, "About Your Commute . . . U.S. Commuting
Statistics. Where Are People Going? How?" IAC Transportation,
July 2008, http://www.slideshare.net/marcus.bowman.slides/
us-commuting-statistical-analysis.

23. Eric M. Weiss, "A Dubious Distinction: The Longest Ride in U.S.," *The
Washington Post*, February 3, 2009, A1.

24. This is based on a 230-day work-year, a 30-year working career
commuting this distance, and an 8-hour workday.

25. Madison Park, "Why We're Sleeping Less," CNNhealth.com, March 6,
2009, CNN, http://www.cnn.com/2009/HEALTH/03/04/sleep.stress
.economy/index.html.

26. Psalm 90:12.

CHAPTER 8—MAINTAINING A WORK-LIFE BALANCE

1. Dan Weikel, "LAX Parking Lot Is Home Away from Home for Airline
Workers," July 20, 2009, http://www.latimes.com/news/local/
la-me-lax-colony20-2009jul20,0,4549617.story.

2. Gene Rudd, MD, and Al Weir, MD, quoting David Allen, MD, *Practice
by the Book: A Christian Doctor's Guide to Living and Serving* (Bristol,
TN: Christian Medical & Dental Associations Resources, 2005), 174.

3. Sylvia Ann Hewlett and Carolyn Buck Luce, "Extreme Jobs: The Dangerous Allure of the 70-Hour Workweek," *Harvard Business Review*, December 2006.

4. Kate Travis, "Work and Life in the Balance," Science Careers from the journal *Science*, December 7, 2007, http://sciencecareers.sciencemag .org/career_magazine/previous_issues/articles/2007_12_07/ caredit.a0700174.

5. Stephen R. Covey, "Work-Life Balance: A Different Cut," Forbes.com, March 3, 2007.

6. Richard A. Swenson, MD, *Margin: Restoring Emotional, Physical, Financial, and Time Reserves to Overloaded Lives* (Colorado Springs, CO: NavPress, 2004), 114.

7. Rhymer Rigby, "Warning: Interruption Overload," *Financial Times*, FT.com, August 23, 2006, http://www.ft.com/cms/s/0/d0f71fb6-3243 -11db-ab06-0000779e2340,dwp_uuid=4e612cca-6707-11da-a650 -0000779e2340,print=yes.html?nclick_check=1.

8. "Ideas from IBM — You've got (too much) mail," October 20, 2008, 2, http://www.ibm.com/ibm/ideasfromibm/us/email/20081020/ IFI_10202008.pdf.

9. Survey of 265 random workers conducted by KRC Research, June 2007.

10. Robert M. Kimmitt, "Why Job Churn Is Good," *The Washington Post*, January 23, 2007, A17.

11. Sophie Bethune, "Stress a Major Health Problem in the U.S., Warns APA," October 24, 2007, http://www.apa.org/releases/stressproblem .html.

12. Hannah Clark, "Getting to No," Forbes.com., March 19, 2007, http:// www.forbes.com/2007/03/19/career-commitment-no-lead-careers -worklife07-cx-hc_0319no.html.

13. Clark, quoting Susan Newman, a social psychologist and author of *The Book of NO*. "In fact, Newman says most people overestimate the fallout from denying a request, and underestimate the consequences of agreeing."

14. Sherry Rauh, "5 Tips for Better Work-Life Balance," *WebMD* Feature,

reviewed November 07, 2006, http://www.webmd.com/balance/guide/5-strategies-for-life-balance.

15. Adrienne Mand, "Slow Down! You Move Too Fast," ABC News, November 1, 2004.

16. Candace Jackson, "The Whirlwind Vacation," *The Wall Street Journal*, February 6, 2009, W1, W4.

17. Charles Dickens, *A Tale of Two Cities* (London: The Macmillan Company, 1922), 382.

18. Trevor Corson, "Simplify, Simplify," *The Atlantic*, April 2009, 26–27.

19. Charles W. Morris and Janet Morris, *Jesus in the Midst of Success* (Nashville: Broadman & Holman, 2000), 85.

20. Jim Loehr and Tony Schwartz, *The Power of Full Engagement: Managing Energy, Not Time, Is the Key to High Performance and Personal Renewal* (New York: Free Press, 2003), 4–5.

21. Swenson, *Margin*, 55.

22. Pew Research Center poll, "Inside the Middle Class: Bad Times Hit the Good Life," April 9, 2008, http://pewsocialtrends.org/pubs/706/middle-class-poll. "Some two-thirds (68%) of middle class respondents say that 'having enough free time to do the things you want' is a very important priority in their lives. That's more than say the same about any other priority we asked about in this survey including: having children (62% said that is very important), being successful in a career (59%), being married (55%), living a religious life (53%), doing volunteer work/donating to charity (52%); and being wealthy (12%). Upper and lower class respondents give essentially the same answers."

23. David Owen, "Rich Man, Poor Man," *Home*, September 1995, 190.

24. Richard A. Swenson, MD, "Chapter 8, Expectation Overload," *The Overload Syndrome: Learning to Live Within Your Limits* (Colorado Springs, CO: NavPress, 1998), 109–121.

25. Shafiga Bakhshaliyeva, "Circus Life: Dancing on the High Wire," *Azerbaijan International* 10, no. 3 (Autumn 2002): 68–69.

26. Elizabeth Goudge, *The Bird in a Tree* (London: Hodder & Stoughton, 1940), 243.

27. "Therefore, as God's chosen people, holy and dearly loved, clothe yourselves with compassion, kindness, humility, gentleness and patience. Bear with each other and forgive whatever grievances you may have against one another. Forgive as the Lord forgave you. And over all these virtues put on love, which binds them all together in perfect unity" (Colossians 3:12-14).

28. Drs. Stevan and Ivonne Hobfoll, *Work Won't Love You Back: The Dual Career Couples Survival Guide*" (New York: W. H. Freeman, 1994), 100.

CHAPTER 9—MEETING THE DECENT MINIMUMS

1. Sylvia Ann Hewlett and Carolyn Buck Luce, "Extreme Jobs: The Dangerous Allure of the 70-Hour Workweek," *Harvard Business Review*, December 2006.

2. For an excellent discussion, see Arlie Russell Hochschild's *Time Bind: When Work Becomes Home and Home Becomes Work* (New York: Metropolitan Books, 1997).

3. Adapted from Richard H. Bube, "On the Pursuit of Excellence: Pitfalls in the Effort to Become No. 1," *Perspectives on Science and Christian Faith*, June 1987, 70–71. Used by permission.

4. Philippians 4:13, Paul writing from prison.

5. Charles W. Morris and Janet Morris, *Jesus in the Midst of Success* (Nashville: Broadman & Holman, 2000), 68.

6. Isaiah 30:21.

7. Haddon Robinson, Plenary Address, Christian Medical & Dental Associations National Meeting, Dallas, Texas, April 29–May 1, 1994.

8. *Children of Men*, movie review from Reel Life Wisdom, http://www .reellifewisdom.com/hope_as_the_sound_of_the_playgrounds _faded_the_despair_set_in_very_odd_what_happens_in_a_world _without_childrens_voices.

9. Mark 10:13-14.

10. Tullian Tchividjian, *Unfashionable: Making a Difference in the World by Being Different* (Colorado Springs, CO: Multnomah, 2009), 27, 8.

11. "I am not saying this because I am in need, for I have learned to be content whatever the circumstances. I know what it is to be in

need, and I know what it is to have plenty. I have learned the secret of being content in any and every situation, whether well fed or hungry, whether living in plenty or in want" (Philippians 4:11-12). "But godliness with contentment is great gain" (1 Timothy 6:6). "Keep your lives free from the love of money and be content with what you have, because God has said, 'Never will I leave you; never will I forsake you'" (Hebrews 13:5).

12. Wendell Berry, "What Are People For?" (New York: North Point Press, 1990), 201.

13. "Therefore, since we are surrounded by such a great cloud of witnesses, let us throw off everything that hinders and the sin that so easily entangles, and let us run with perseverance the race marked out for us" (Hebrews 12:1).

14. Gene Rudd, MD, and Al Weir, MD, quoting David Allen, MD, *Practice by the Book: A Christian Doctor's Guide to Living and Serving* (Bristol, TN: Christian Medical & Dental Associations Resources, 2005), 180.

15. "Therefore do not worry about tomorrow, for tomorrow will worry about itself. Each day has enough trouble of its own" (Matthew 6:34).

16. "Do not be anxious about anything, but in everything, by prayer and petition, with thanksgiving, present your requests to God. And the peace of God, which transcends all understanding, will guard your hearts and your minds in Christ Jesus" (Philippians 4:6-7). "Peace I leave with you; my peace I give you. I do not give to you as the world gives. Do not let your hearts be troubled and do not be afraid" (John 14:27). "Do not fret because of evil men or be envious of those who do wrong; for like the grass they will soon wither, like green plants they will soon die away. Trust in the LORD and do good; dwell in the land and enjoy safe pasture. Delight yourself in the LORD and he will give you the desires of your heart. Commit your way to the LORD; trust in him and he will do this: He will make your righteousness shine like the dawn, the justice of your cause like the noonday sun. Be still before the LORD and wait patiently for him; do not fret when men succeed in their ways, when they carry out their wicked schemes. Refrain from anger and turn from wrath; do not fret—it leads only to evil" (Psalm 37:1-8).

17. "Two are better than one, because they have a good return for their work: If one falls down, his friend can help him up. But pity the man who falls and has no one to help him up!" (Ecclesiastes 4:9-10).
18. Rudyard Kipling, *The Glory of the Garden*, 1911.
19. Acts 20:35.
20. John 1:16.

CHAPTER 10—SECURING A SPACE FOR DEEP
CONSECUTIVE THOUGHTS

1. Psalm 42:11.
2. Michio Kaku, *The Theory Behind the Equation*, PBS.org, http://www .pbs.org/wgbh/nova/einstein/kaku.html. This material from Kaku's book *Einstein's Cosmos: How Albert Einstein's Vision Transformed Our Understanding of Space and Time* (New York: Norton, 2004), 60–63.
3. "Tech Makes Working Harder, Not Easier," Reuters, CNET News.com. February 24, 2006.
4. "Ideas from IBM—You've got (too much) mail," October 20, 2008, 2, http://www.ibm.com/ibm/ideasfromibm/us/email/20081020/ IFI_10202008.pdf.
5. Lucius Annaeus Seneca, "On the Shortness of Life," section 7, translated by John W. Basore, Corpus Scriptorum Latinorum, http:// www.forumromanum.org/literature/seneca_younger/brev_e.html.
6. Charles Swindoll, *Intimacy with the Almighty* (Dallas: Word, 1996), 9–10, 42.
7. Tom Peters, "Please, I just need some quite time," *Forbes ASAP*, October 4, 1999, 37.
8. Ravi Zacharias Ministry, January 23, 2009, citing Mark Edmundson, "Dwelling in Possibilities," *The Chronicle of Higher Education* 54, no. 27, B7.
9. Søren Kierkegaard, quoted in Gilbert Meilaender's "Progress Without Pause," *First Things*, February 2009.
10. William Everson, "The Wise," *The Veritable Years, Poems 1949–1966* (Boston: Black Sparrow Press, 1978), 14.

INDEX

ABOUT THE AUTHOR

RICHARD A. SWENSON, MD, is a physician-futurist, best-selling author, and award-winning educator. He received his BS in physics (Phi Beta Kappa) from Denison University (1970) and his MD from the University of Illinois School of Medicine (1974). Following five years of private practice, in 1982 Dr. Swenson accepted a teaching position as associate clinical professor with the University of Wisconsin medical school system Department of Family Medicine, where he taught for fifteen years. He currently is a full-time futurist, physician-researcher, author, and educator. As a physician, his focus is "cultural medicine," researching the intersection of health and culture. As a futurist, his emphasis is fourfold: the future of the world system, Western culture, faith, and health care.

Dr. Swenson has traveled extensively (to fifty-five countries, living abroad for a total of three years), including a year of study in Europe and medical work in developing countries. He is the author of seven books, including the best-selling *Margin: Restoring Emotional, Physical, Financial, and Time Reserves to Overloaded Lives* and *The Overload Syndrome: Learning to Live Within Your Limits*, both award winning.

He has written and presented widely, both nationally and internationally, on the themes of margin, stress, overload, life balance, complexity, societal change, health care, and future trends. A representative listing of presentations include a wide variety of career, professional, educational, governmental, and management groups; most major church denominations and organizations; members of the United Nations, Congress, NASA, and the Pentagon. He was an invited guest participant for the 44th Annual National Security Seminar.

Dr. Swenson has given presentations to national medical conferences such as the American Academy of Family Physicians, the American Association of Occupational Medicine, the American Society of Prospective Medicine, the general medical staff of the Mayo Clinic, as well as hundreds of other national, regional, state, and local medical settings. He also has researched extensively and written on the future of health care, helping to initiate a national multidisciplinary group examining the healthcare crisis and exploring new paradigms. In 2002, he was awarded the National Leadership Award from the Central States Occupational Medical Association for his original work on margin and overload. In 2003, he was awarded Educator of the Year Award by Christian Medical and Dental Associations.

Dr. Swenson and his wife, Linda, live in Menomonie, Wisconsin. They have two sons, Matthew (and Suzie) and Adam (and Maureen), and a granddaughter, Katja.

Restore balance with these titles from Dr. Richard A. Swenson.

Margin
Richard A. Swenson, MD
978-1-57683-682-8

Margin is the space that once existed between ourselves and our limits. If you yearn for relief from the pain and pressure of overload, take a lifelong dose of *Margin*. This book offers the benefits of good health, financial stability, fulfilling relationships, and availability for God's purposes that will follow you all of your days.

A Minute of Margin
Richard A. Swenson, MD
978-1-57683-068-0

Rediscover the space you need in between your work, your schedule, and your limits by eliminating unneeded frustrations and reflecting on how you spend your time. This devotional's 180 daily readings offer encouragement, healing, and rest as you deal with time management, stress, and busyness.

Restoring Margin to Overloaded Lives
Richard A. Swenson, MD
978-1-57683-184-7

Are you lacking the time, money, or energy to accomplish the tasks of a given week or month? Then you're headed for system failure. Whether you're facing burnout now or want to prevent it, these eleven lessons can help you understand stress and limits, find balance and rest, and maintain priorities.

Still experiencing chaos?
Let Dr. Swenson show you how to
overcome the busyness of life.